CULTURAL (
UNDERSTANDING AND DEVELOPING YOUR
ORGANIZATIONAL CULTURE

Dr. Andrew K. Fox

ENDORSEMENTS

A foundational component of taking a company from good to great is the culture that is established by the company's leadership. Today's leaders are challenged more than ever with creating, blending, and nurturing the organization's culture to create a competitive advantage. Andrew is a person of conscientious thought that will, with a historical backdrop, take you on a journey that challenges you to deeply assess your own approach to establishing a winning culture.

Mark Eiland
Managing Partner
TMV Business Group

One reason that there are so many different theories and publications about organizational culture is that different authors and researchers focus on different elements. Most, if not all, of these books lack a concern with organizational dynamics. In Dr. Andrew Fox's new book, he focuses on organizational dynamics. The book explains that companies must find their cultural clarity, their values, and their purpose. This can help drive actions, strategy, how employees behave, and how choices and decisions are made.

William Böll
Co-Founder
Nvolve Technologies

Dr. Fox takes the road less traveled and departs from the false hope of traditional management systems designed to reinforce culture as he drives upstream to the interview process. There he looks to explore and discover a cultural fit at the point of hire, given culture is more than half shaped at that point. New to me is the idea of a cultural adaptor, becoming a leader in embracing change and adapting to an ever-changing world and culture. Dr. Fox's supposition is in order to remain relevant, we must be becoming curious, avoid being judgmental, prepare for mistakes, pursue support, and pause to reflect. These and many other insights were birthed from decades of Dr. Fox's cultural curiosity and will fast forward any organization into cultural clarity!

Steve Leach
President
Acacia Strategic Advisors

Over the last year, I have anxiously watched my business colleague, published author, international speaker, and most importantly, friend, Dr. Andrew Fox pour his more than thirty years of professional experience into his company eloquently and appropriately called Cultural Clarity. Today, the seeds sifted, planted, and nurtured decades ago have borne insightful fruit and a bounty worthy of sharing with businesses, schools, churches, and non-profits. Understanding provides clarity. Possessing that knowledge and the ability to leverage its potential is the key to optimizing an organization's health, resiliency, and culture. The time will always be right for cultural clarity.

Michael Francis
Founder
BEAM Executive Advisors

Dr. Fox's *Cultural Clarity* provides insightful background and challenging reflection that help those in leadership address the question, "Are we getting the results we set out to get? If not, why not?" You and your organization can't afford not to explore these below-the-surface questions around organizational culture.

Carol Peters-Tanksley, M.D., D.Min.
Author, speaker, clinical professor

Dr. Fox brings a voice of conviction and clarity into the conversation of organizational culture that is fresh and needed. His no-nonsense approach to honest evaluation and relentless commitment to answer difficult questions puts you in the best possible place to move your organization forward and thrive in the process. If you're looking to unlock the full potential of your leadership and of the organization you lead, this book is for you!

Josh Jamison
Lead Pastor
Eastridge Church
Sammamish, WA

Dietrich Bonhoeffer once said, "The time when people could be told everything by means of words is over." Dr Andrew Fox shoots past the words and provides the ingredients a person needs toward creating cultural clarity. Words only can go so far; sometimes a person needs practical steps to navigate unknown waters and territory. Dr Fox, in his book, gives context to the history of organizational clarity and then provides boots for you, helps you lace them up, and gets you on the ground, marching forward like a soldier on a mission. This is a book every person in leadership needs to put on their shelf whether you are building, transitioning, or starting a business. This book and practicality are refreshing!

Jeff Thorp
Lead Pastor
Ember Church
Bellevue, WA

Dr. Fox provides a historical foundation to understanding organizational culture as well as the influences of subcultures that your people bring with them to work and how subculture can contribute to the success of your organization. We are deeply grateful for the interactive element of the book and how the questions allow the reader to reflect on their leadership style.

Rev. Dr. Nathan J. Robertson Jr.
Executive Pastor
St. James Missionary Baptist Church
Austin, TX

As the church moves beyond COVID-19, there are some longings to return to 'normal'. However, previous normality is forever lost. *Cultural Clarity* provides insights and practices that will assist in establishing, articulating, and implementing a culture that will keep your organization agile and thriving. You will want to read this book at least once a year.

Rev. Dr. Tim Adour
Church of the Revelation
The Bronx, NY

CULTURAL CLARITY

UNDERSTANDING AND
DEVELOPING YOUR
ORGANIZATIONAL
CULTURE

ANDREW K. FOX

Summary: This book brings clarity to the highest priority among executive leaders today: organizational culture. Picture organizational culture like adhesive holding everything together. This adhesive focuses on how things get done rather than what gets done. It shapes the relationships and behavior of every member on every level. So, organizational culture can be referred to as the silent code of conduct, background aura, or white noise, yet it impacts everyone in the organization, especially new hires.

Publication date: April 2022

ISBN Print: 978-1-7340733-1-7
ISBN eBook: 978-1-7340733-2-4

Library of Congress Control Number: 2022937077

1. Culture 2. Organizations 3. Hiring 4. Leadership 5. Competitive 6. Success 7. Adapting 8. Corporations

I Fox, Andrew K.   II Cultural Clarity

Cultural Clarity may be purchased at special quantity discounts for organizations colleges to be used for educational purposes.

For more information or to have Dr. Fox speak at your event: andrew@culturalclarity.us or (512) 897-7886

Proofreader: Annie K. Preston
Editor: Tracy Johnson
Cover and Interior Layout and Design: Lynne Hopwood

Contact Andrew for Reprints of specific chapters or the entire book and Rights, or Licensing Agreements

Publisher: Oxford Publishing
Website: www.culturalclarity.us

Printed in the United States of America

DEDICATION

To my wife Renee.
The most loving, giving, and endearing human being I know.

PREFACE

How did I get here and why write this book?

The answer to the first question is failure and success, pain and joy, disappointment and satisfaction, frustration and clarity, anxiety and peace, and— the paradoxical human experiences are seemingly endless.

But that's my point.

In a world of perpetuating smoke and mirrors that create the illusional image of a successful career and life, I arrived at where I am by allowing the conundrum of experiences to positively shape who I am today. More so, it developed a greater capacity in my life for people and how they function in organizational culture.

And that's my point in answering the second question.

The negative experiences caused me to ask the right questions. So, I entered a conversation with good friends that lasted several years. What emerged was not obvious but most surprising. Friends in positions of leadership from municipal organizations, corporations, colleges and universities, startup businesses, non-profits, and churches clearly saw what evaded me.

Throughout my career I had been hired to positions of leadership by organizations that were in crisis, or wanting something done that seemed impossible, or at best highly improbable. Before the idea of organizational culture became a priority in today's marketplace, I naturally developed what needed to be done by focusing on the culture of an organization.

This is my passion and why I wrote this book.

Your organizational culture is like adhesive that holds everything together. I want to help you discover what adds to the adhesiveness of your organization and what dilutes its power to bring your people, processes, business strategy, and structure together.

After reading this book, take the complimentary self-test on my website to see what your organizational culture currently looks like. If you're serious about the culture of your organization, take the Cultural Clarity Comprehensive Test©. Schedule an online meeting with me at no cost to you.

I really am looking forward to meeting you!

www.culturalclarity.us

ACKNOWLEDGMENTS

I want to acknowledge the extraordinary debt I owe to people who dedicated portions of their life to being curious. From people whose very bones have turned to dust and others who passed away in my lifetime, to those who continue to be inquisitive by asking the right questions.

Their observations, findings, acquired knowledge, methods—all encased in the human experience we called emotions—are the immeasurable treasures they offer all of us today. Physical libraries, archives, rich conversations late into the night, and an eternity of catalogued information at my fingertips online give me pause to say:

Thank you for your curiosity.

CONTENTS

List of Figures:

FOREWORD

Culture is something we make.

Either accidentally or intentionally, we are always culturing those around us, tending to their expectations, reactions, and aspirations. We raise our children more through our relationships than through our rules, and we form lasting friendships in the same way. If so, organizational culture cannot be ignored in the workplace.

Culture comes from the Latin word "colere" which means "to tend." Originally the term was used to describe cultivating soil but later developed to include the cultivation of the mind, the economy, the arts, and so on. We tend to that which lives in the ground, in ourselves, and in our world. We are cultured, and we create culture in turn.

When cultivating agriculture, we want to ensure all we produce can grow. Will it be healthy? Rich? Flavorful? Will people from outside our region hear the rumors of our quality and travel to see for themselves? Likewise, we want to cultivate an organizational environment in which our people are strong, thriving, and much celebrated. We want to grow our business and brand to such excellence that customers and clients pursue us rather than the other way around.

And the good news is that a healthy culture is something you can create. Once you learn the essential ingredients, you can monitor your culture and tend to it, ensuring it grows into something of which you can be proud and which will produce a spectacular yield.

There is no better motivator than a thriving culture. There is no better attraction than an environment of passion and energy. There is no more profitable strategy—for doing more with less—

than investing in the workplace, ensuring everyone has everything they need to grow.

Eighteenth-century writer and entomologist, John Abbot, once proclaimed that "Every man's ability may be strengthened or increased by culture." He was not wrong. When we bring our people together, synergizing their aptitude, their intelligence, and their drive, our momentum and output dramatically increase.

And it's fun!

Remember, we're not just trying to get every ounce of possible productivity out of the people we employ. We don't want them exhausted, fragile, or lifeless. Such lack of care hardly produces sustainable results, let alone legacy yield. No—we want to care for our people in such a way that their well-being and happiness energize their tasks and enliven the workplace.

Read on for keen insights from a well-respected professional who wants to show you how.

Dr. David McDonald
Founder and President at Fossores Chapter House
Jackson, Michigan

INTRODUCTION

I'm sure you've heard the following statement before, but it's well worth repeating simply because it pervades everything about your organization: "Culture eats strategy for breakfast."[1] This book recognizes the enduring impact and increased influence of organizational culture. The material is a contemporary response to why the culture of your own organization is more important than the strategy of your business. More so, it is a practical guide to developing the culture of your organization by engaging you with questions to answer. So, grab something to write with!

The book is contextualized in my own career, spanning three decades and experience in twenty-eight different countries. I want you to know that in advance with respect to your time invested in reading the material. Now, I'm not a theorist but a practitioner. I want you to know that too. Here are the four reasons that underpin my passion and practice in organizational culture:

First, though I earned a master's degree in leadership and a PhD in intercultural studies, practical and ongoing education always occurs in the field of experience and not the classroom. Academic degrees can be nothing but short-lived bragging rights unless they are applied in meaningful ways to where people live, work, play, worship, and mature through life. Another quote you will know that is equally worth repeating sums up my first reason: "It is not the critic who counts; not the man who points out how the strong man stumbles, or where the doer of deeds could have done them better. The credit belongs to the man who is actually in

---

[1] Attributed to Peter Drucker (1909–2005) the Austrian-American educator, author, and consultant who contributed to the practical and philosophical foundations of business corporations.

the arena…"[2] I want you to know this book comes from the arena of ongoing experience supported by valid and reliable research.

Second, I learn a great deal from leaders in a dialogical approach. This simply means that mutual learning and understanding takes place between myself and clients. However, what I bring to the table of young leaders is over thirty years of experience affording me insights in how organizational culture has developed over time. The first chapter of this book will take you through a brief history of organizational culture beginning in the 1800s. Today, the culture of any organization has become far more intrinsic beyond a skills or personality test that used to define culture at work. I want you to know that I went through the changes and adaptations that were necessary to succeed, and I continue to enjoy adjusting in today's world. So,

> The book is contextualized in my own career, spanning three decades and experience in twenty-eight different countries.

this book is not about imposing ideas from yesteryear but as Mark Parker said about Nike, "We have a culture where we are incredibly self-critical, we don't get comfortable with our success."[3]

Third, organizations of any kind have much in common. For instance, hiring practices involve the central idea of being a cultural fit, and onboarding new hires is not just a process but an exhibition of organizational culture. As culture develops, established members in any organization need opportunities to become cultural adaptors. If you are in a position of leadership, you must be willing to hire and fire based on a cultural fit or adaptation: "If you're willing to do that, then you're well on your way to building a company culture that is in line with the brand you want to build."[4] While profitability is another commonality among or-

---

[2] President Teddy Roosevelt (1858–1919) speech called "Citizenship in the Republic" delivered in Sorbonne, Paris, April 23, 1910, at 3:00 p.m. but retitled "The Man in the Arena."

[3] Mark Parker, CEO of Nike, 2006–2020.

[4] Tony Hsieh, CEO of Zappos, 1999–2020.

ganizations, how that bottom line is achieved is very different for each type of organization. For example, businesses achieve profitability through the sale of their services or products; schools through enrollment, retention, and graduation; and churches through volunteerism and donations.[5] I want you to know this book is not about management systems, the latest technology, or marketing strategies. It is about the underpinning and overarching power and influence of organizational culture that holds everything together in your organization.

Fourth, I was born in England where I lived, worked, played, and worshipped for the first thirty-one years of my life (and where I met my wife). The United States has been our home for over two decades where we raised our three children. The twenty-eight different countries I visited to work, observe, and research helped me to understand how organizational culture functions in such a way where people flourish, or as Brian Kristofek summarized, "Being a great place to work is the difference between being a good company and a great company."[6] You will find a variety of principles in this book that will make your organization a great place to work.

The fourth reason is important to me for a single reason. More than any other country I have visited, the population of the United States where I now live is by far the greatest representation of global cultures. Consequently, organizational culture in America involves subcultures far more than organizations in any other country.[7] This book will help you understand the influence of subcultures that your people bring with them to work, and how subculture can positively contribute to the overall success of your organization. Again, I want you to know that my observations and research are not clinical from a classroom, but face to face, shoulder to shoulder, with people in the field of experience.

These are my four reasons I want you to know that contextualized my passion and practice in organizational culture. What

---

[5] Often called ministry and tithes or an offering, but in organizational terms is volunteerism and donations.

[6] Brian Kristofek, president and CEO, Upshot (2022).

[7] Pew Research, "Key Findings about U.S. Immigrants," 2020.

follows will help you realize just how enduring and impacting the familiar statement is that "Culture eats strategy for breakfast," not just in terms of information, but more so in what is currently occurring in your own organization.

My hope is that you will come out of any element of cultural chaos in your organization, make cultural corrections, recommence the cultural journey, and move into cultural conversion as a living experience of Simon Sinek's words, "Customers will never love a company until the employees love it first."[8]

Now, let's look at a brief history to understand the present and the developing future.

---

[8] Simon Sinek, optimist and British-American author on Twitter, April 16, 2014, at 4:33 p.m.

PART ONE:

A BRIEF HISTORY OF ORGANIZATIONAL CULTURE

"The most important events in every age never reach the history books."

(C.S. Lewis, *The Dark Tower*, 1938, 17)

The history of organizational culture is both useful and informative to understand how culture functions in organizations today. But whose history? Through what lens is this particular history explored? I must acknowledge there is more than one view that can be traced, therefore, more than one history of organizational culture. Therefore, I will keep to a brief history that focuses on the West, more so, Great Britain and the United States. I must emphasize its briefness as this is not a history book. The idea of this chapter is to trace the breadcrumbs from the 1800s to the present day. And Lewis was correct, the unfolding events of part one were not found in history books.

Even with a focus on the West, and particularly in Britain and America, we find a variety of shades attached to the lens from the expertise of economists, sociologists, anthropologists, ecclesiologists, educationalists, and literalists that color (even taint) what this chapter seeks to trace. So, I'm adopting the culturist lens as one "who emphasizes the importance of culture in determining behavior and the way in which it functions."[9] I've been called many things in my life (humorous, sarcastic, and vicious), but for the sake of this chapter let's go with culturist. Also, to keep this chapter lively and engaging, I'm going to draw upon classic stories you will have read, or at least are familiar with, that paint a picture.

[9] lexico.com/en/definition/culturalist.

CHAPTER ONE

1800S: THE DICKENSIAN WORLD

Let's begin with blatant honesty. Researchers in the 1800s rarely used the word "culture" in their examination of organizations, but they did rely on sociological and anthropological concepts and methods, so we can say they conducted research into organizational culture.[10] We can also say the 1800s was the cusp of the Industrial Revolution. New manufacturing processes transitioned from hand production to machinery as iron production increased. It was against this period of change in the workforce that Charles Dickens wrote his popular novels.

In many ways, the time we now call Dickensian had a distinct paternalistic approach to employees as "family." Employers provided a variety of benefits that included company housing, stores, libraries, schools, churches, and in some cases sports and entertainment. They were called "company towns"[11] because the organization owned everything. Admittedly, company towns were popular in the US, considering railroad construction sites, lumber camps, turpentine camps, and coal mines were at a considerable distance from the nearest town.

---

[10] Harrison M. Trice and Janice M. Beyer, *The Cultures of Work Organizations*, Pearson, 1992.

[11] Merriam-Webster 2022: "a community that is dependent on one firm for all or most of the necessary services or functions of town life."

In Britain, locations like Copley (1849) and Saltaire (1853) started as company towns, prompting the creation of many more across the country. For instance, Port Sunlight (1888) in Cheshire was established by Lord Leverhulme manufacturing soap and tallow. Leverhulme provided the workers with a complete way of life.

The Cadbury brothers established Bournville (1895) away from the city of Birmingham, believing that an improved environment would increase productivity. They were not wrong. Building schools and training facilities, Cadbury wanted their workers educated and up to date with the latest machinery. Much like professions today that require so may hours per year in ongoing education, the Cadbury brothers were ahead of the game. Added to this were the social elements of sports, clubs, and societies all owned by the Cadbury brothers. Now, this may sound utopian, but understand that executives in these large companies were very much in control of company towns. More so, the religion of the executives was the pervading religious practice.

Smaller organizations could not offer their employees such holistic packages, but they were kind, inclusive, and generous toward the well-being of their employees. We see this in Charles Dickens' *A Christmas Carol* (1843) where Mr. Fezziwig—the proprietor of a warehouse business—threw a great Christmas party for his employees. Dickens was conveying a set of communal values and a way of life in the workplace, but like many of his novels portray, these values quickly gave way through the 1800s.

> In many ways, the time we now call Dickensian had a distinct paternalistic approach to employees as "family."

Many organizations abandoned their benevolent attitude toward the well-being of workers, becoming blatantly exploitative and abusive even in the company towns.[12] Ironically, Ebenezer Scrooge learned his trade where employees were treated as family but then went on to be the exploiter before he was visited by his

---

[12] S. M. Jacoby, *Employing Bureaucracy*, University Press, 1985.

recently deceased and penitent partner, Marley. Ironically, Dickens names the crooked character Fagin in his *A Christmas Carol* after a boy called Bob Fagin he worked with as a child in a blacking factory. I guess some memories never fade.

His novel *Hard Times* (1854) is distinctly written against the backdrop of the Industrial Revolution, particularly highlighting the exploitation of women and children in extreme unhealthy conditions. Mechanical manufacturing was on the rise, but small hands were still needed for manual tasks, and in the Dickensian world there were no better hands than women and their children. Dickens was challenging the sacrifice of hard working and loyal people for the sake of progress. So, in order to write *Hard Times*, he visited cotton mills where 30,000 people labored across the country. What he found gave voice to the characters in his novel, particularly the silver-tongued Slackbridge who manipulated both the workers and management for his own gain.

Summary

When we think about employers calling their members family today, the dangers that give way to exploitation and abuse in the 1800s are highly regulated. On one hand, the company towns offered over 200 years ago far outweigh the packaged deals of today. On the other hand, today's salaries are far higher. We are far more private and independent outside of the workplace than the 1800s and much more in control of our retirement or investment funds.

Many organizations abandoned their benevolent attitude toward the well-being of workers, becoming blatantly exploitative and abusive even in the company towns.

Let's close the door on the Dickensian world and look into the first half of a new millennium.

CHAPTER TWO

1900–1950: PERVADING HIGH, UPPER, AND LOWER CLASSES

What evolved from patristic approaches were formal organizational structures that included levels of supervision, rules, compensation systems, evaluations, and disciplinary procedures.[13] It's not that a family environment disappeared, and structures appeared, but changes in society meant employers had declining influence in the company town they built.

Toad of Toad Hall in the 1910s

In many ways, a limitation on the domestic lives of workers served to reinforce the class system within the workplace. Anyone familiar with Kenneth Grahame's *Wind in the Willows* (1908) will quickly see his narrative is written against the background of a changing social and class system by championing the underdog. The characters called Badger, Ratty, and Mole are celebrated, whereas Toad represents the despised higher class of the elite. So, internal

> So, internal methods in organizations increased in the early 1900s where the ruling class could control employee behavior while at work

---

[13] C. I. Bernard, *The Functions of the Executive*, Harvard University Press, 1938.

methods in organizations increased in the early 1900s where the ruling class could control employee behavior while at work, but not always at home like the 1800s.

Jeeves and Wooster in the 1920s

After WWI, the 1920s saw a huge movement toward incentive pay schemes by intentionally observing and interviewing employees, rewarding them for what they were worth to the organization. Stanley Mathewson from the National Labor Relations Board documented research involving 105 organizations with surprising results.[14] He showed massive restriction in the productivity of employees if every moment of their work was not strictly organized. Some worked at a leisurely pace while others took a nap during the day or ambled around. Contrary to William Penn's alleged statement, "Men must be governed by God, or they will be ruled by tyrants,"[15] Mathewson found that God's governance at work was not as strict as a good foreman. In short, employees were not to be left to their own initiative. Think about this while reflecting on today's practices where initiative is paramount to success. It was this background of workers being governed by upper and higher classes that P.G. Woodhouse lampooned in his books about a butler called Jeeves and his employer called Bertie Wooster (1923).

In order to further understand behavior of employees, more research was conducted from 1924–1927.[16] Researchers wanted to know if environmental influences could change behavior and increase productivity. Surprisingly, better lighting was certainly a winner, but this single variable in the workplace left the study inconclusive. Far more exterior factors contributed to a thriving environment than good lighting. What's surprising is no research focused on the relational aspect of executives, managers, and the workers.

---

[14] Stanley B. Mathewson, *Restriction of Output Among Unorganized Workers*, Viking Press, 1931.

[15] Attributed to William Penn (1644–1718), but no one is quite sure if he actually said this.

[16] National Research Council of the Academy of Social Sciences at the Western Electric Hawthorne in the publication of F. J. Roethlisberger and W. J. Dickson, *Management and the Worker*, Harvard University Press, 1939, 14–18.

In 1927, psychologist Elton Mayo began his studies measuring the impact of taking breaks, eating snacks, working hours in a day, and working days in the week.[17] His findings were also inconclusive, so he began to investigate the impact on productivity through wage incentives.[18] Once more, what he found was inconclusive. In both cases, inconclusiveness pointed to the possibility of other factors influencing a thriving and productive environment. We must remember that in the 1920s researchers did not know what we take for granted today. It was a decade of executives learning how to communicate with the workers through their managers, and the workers understanding what executives wanted interpreted by managers. Even so, no investigation considered the relational aspects of executives, managers, and workers, even though it was the elephant in the room.

In 1928, inductive studies were carried out by interviewing employees for thirty minutes asking what they liked and disliked about their jobs.[19] It was a fact-finding initiative. In each case, the employees would discuss matters unrelated to the questions. When corrected, each would return to matters they wanted to discuss about their day-to-day work. So, the researchers changed their inductive approach to a less direct method. The results were more cathartic, as facts gave way to sentiment. It appeared that sharing concerns tended to lift the spirit of employees.

Sentiment was something significant to focus on if increased productivity was desired.[20] We can look back to the late 1920s, scratching our heads in bemusement because employee well-being is something we fully embrace today. But during this era the difficult tension of fact-sentiment needed developing against the background of a ridged Jeeves and Wooster class system. Furthermore, something called "the informal organization"

---

[17] Ibid., 19–186.

[18] National Research Council of the Academy of Social Sciences at the Western Electric Hawthorne in the publication of F. J. Roethlisberger and W. J. Dickson, *Management and the Worker*, Harvard University Press, 1939, 128–160.

[19] F. J. Roethlisberger and W. J. Dickson, *Management and the Worker*, Harvard University Press, 1939, 189–376.

[20] Ibid., 282.

emerged in the findings of researchers, or what we call a "subculture" today.[21]

Orient Express in the 1930s

The workers' subcultures tended to rely on each other for support by distancing themselves from managers. Providing support for the workers through informal organization (subculture) was unofficial, but it was a tangible vehicle for managers to hear the concerns of the workers.

In order to sanction something that was already happening, executives initiated counseling programs to address the sentiment of workers. Over time counseling services evolved into human relations, arriving at human resources today.[22] Again, we take much for granted but back in the 1930s—even with American labor unions benefiting from the New Deal policies of Franklin D. Roosevelt—an executive was typically from a higher class, managers from middle to upper class, and the labor force from the working class. Think of Agatha Christie's *Murder on the Orient Express* (1934) to grasp the idea of a three-tiered class system within one organization, or in this case, a train with first-class, second-class, and third-class carriages.

> The higher class were considered the brain, while the upper class management were thought of as a nervous system, and lower class workers the actual body parts.

It was the anthropologist Eliot Dismore Chapple who introduced the idea of people working together in an organization as a "living organism."[23] The higher class were considered the brain, while the upper class management were thought of as a nervous

[21] Ibid., 379–548.

[22] W. J. Dickson and F. J. Roethlisberger, *Counseling in an Organization*, Harvard University Press, 1966.

[23] E. D. Chapple, *Organization Problems in Industry*, Applied Anthropology 1(4), 2–9, 1941.

system, and lower class workers the actual body parts.[24] Much like the human body, understanding an organization like a living organism meant equilibrium was essential for productivity. Thus, Chapple went on to coin the phrase "anthropological engineering" as a significant step toward understanding the equilibrium of an organization—or the balance between executives, management, and the workers.[25] If there was a disruption in the organization, the "brain" would take care of it. What became clearer during this decade was a greater understanding of how the social system functioned in the workplace through subcultures. We also see this in how British and American military ranks functioned going into WWII.

Big Family Solutions in the 1940s

It was in the 1940s that Sears attempted to synergize the beliefs and values of all employees into corporate strategy, formal organization, and informal organizations (or subcultures).[26] As much as this sounds back to front, the attempt was to help locate where problems arose, and then deal with them where they occurred. This way, higher levels of management—or the "brain"— did not have to become involved. Much like Frank and Ernestine Gilbreth's *Cheaper by the Dozen* (1948), Sears was one of the first organizations that adopted a pseudo-family approach. As the characters Tom and Kate Barker organized all their children to deal with problems, Sears believed those involved in causing a problem must be included in the resolution for the family to succeed. Though a little utopian, it was a good stride toward how organizational culture functions today.

---

[24] B. B. Gardner, *Human Relations in Industry*, Irwin Inc., 1945.

[25] E. D. Chapple, *Anthropological Engineering: Its Use to Administrators*, Applied Anthropology 3(1), 23–32, 1943.

[26] D. G. Moore, *Managerial Strategies and Organization in Sears Retailing*, Dissertation, University of Chicago, 1954.

Anxiety in the 1950s

Post WWII, more inductive studies were carried out through the 1950s where interaction and sentiment were analyzed. For example, sociologist William Foote Whyte studied sentiment among the workforce at Inland Steel, concluding that ignoring how employees feel would always result in a strike of some sort.[27] Through his interviewing method, key words like "trust" and "no confidence" were frequently used, not based on pure fact, but the sentiment of employees.[28] The mess that Whyte stumbled on was that if employees were given a measure of power to say what they wanted without threat of termination, they tended to exert it.[29] Hands down, this was groundbreaking in terms of organizational culture.

> The mess that Whyte stumbled on was that if employees were given a measure of power to say what they wanted without threat of termination, they tended to exert it.

By now, counseling services had fully evolved into human relations. Researchers argued that managers should listen to their employees and involve them to some degree in the decision-making process. When we consider what was happening back in the early 1900s, the idea of listening to the workforce had come a long way. However, executives generally continued to manage in the same old way throughout the 1950s, so very little improvement was made in a working relationship between executives, managers, and the workforce. It was a period that W.H. Auden famously predicted would be *The Age of Anxiety* (1947) where all forms of authority and hierarchy would be questioned. And in a post-WWII decade it was expressed in the world of music, in particular rock and roll.

---

[27] W. F. Whyte, *Pattern for Industrial Peace*, Harper and Brothers, 1951.

[28] Ibid., 232.

[29] A. W. Gouldner, *Wildcat Strike*, Harper & Row, 1954.

Summary

The first half of the 1900s takes us from the declining control of company towns all the way through to the importance of how people feel at work, or how they interpret their experiences. In the 1910s, the class system was highlighted in the workplace; the 1920s people worked best when strictly managed; 1930s external environmental improvements were considered; 1940s the sentiment of employees mattered; and yet, by the 1950s little research had been done on communication between executives (higher class), managers (upper class), and the workers (lower class).

However, the 1960s would bring about the start of a revolution in organizational culture. Let's take a look at this in the next chapter.

CHAPTER THREE

1960–1990: LEARNING TO COMMUNICATE ORGANIZATIONAL CULTURE

Whether Auden's predictions about the 1950s were true or not, what followed in the 1960s was, in many ways, the embodiment of the American dream. It allowed for a good salary to support a family and an independent lifestyle with room for advancement.

> what followed in the 1960s was, in many ways, the embodiment of the American dream.

Etiquette of Mad Men in the 1960s

From today's perspective, it did look hierarchical with a strict code of etiquette among all employees. Nevertheless, such etiquette gave way to drinking, smoking, and socializing on the job as a common practice. Some would even say it was encouraged. A cursory read of the *Mad Men* novels[30] by little-known author T. W. Senduhran shows how the complexities of etiquette, strict codes, and socializing worked as a somewhat hypocritical behavior at work, especially for married men.

---

[30] Made for TV ACM (2007–2015).

When Amy Vanderbilt published her *Complete Book of Etiquette: A Guide to Gracious Living* (1954), she brought to the public's attention how structure and expectations defined corporate culture. Chapter 20 of her book is titled "Man's Manners in the Business World." Quoting an excerpt from it will show two things: 1) how misogynistic corporate life really was, and 2) the enduring matters of presentation and personal conduct:

"Young men who want to become executive material must do more than apply themselves to the technique of their jobs. They must school themselves in social as well as business manners if they want to get ahead. They must learn how to dress, how to conduct themselves on various social and business occasions and how to communicate their ideas to others in concise, well-chosen language. We have all known successful businessmen whose grammar was bad, whose taste in clothes was atrocious, and who broke every rule of good manners, if indeed they knew any existed. The great corporations invariably practice a most formal business etiquette. Their façade is imposing, they employ well-dressed, soft-spoken receptionists, they provide private offices and interoffice communications to cut down on noise and traffic. They usually exercise considerable control over the behavior and appearance of their employees."

Again, from today's perspective, Vanderbilt does sound like a snob. But ask yourself, how much of her proposed etiquette is still functioning today?

Hitchhiker's Guide in the 1970s

Decreasing research in the 1960s about work behaviors did not prove fruitful in America. For example, in the 1970s the American economy faced what economists called "stagflation."[31] This phrase combined inflation and economic stagnation depicting the haunting image of unemployment. These conditions were especially problematic for American commentators because they contrasted so starkly with the experience of the Japanese economy which had continued to prosper throughout the same period.

---

[31] Martin L. Weitzman, *The Share Economy: Conquering Stagflation*, Harvard University Press, 1984.

Now, I don't want to wander off into the land of the economist but keep to the path of the culturist. Enough to say that when researchers developed identical surveys carried out in Japan and America, the results were different because the underlying assumptions of the questions in both countries were very different. If you want to grasp how different those assumptions were (and still are), think about Douglas Adams' *Hitchhiker's Guide to the Galaxy* (1979). Put yourself in the shoes (or slippers) of Arthur Dent meeting Ford Prefect from a small planet in the vicinity of Betelgeuse. The assumptions about life, authority, responsibility, and community of both characters are not the same. So, when people talk about a global economy, we must consider that national cultures see things differently.

American Psycho in the 1980s

By the early 1980s the actual phrase "organizational culture" caught the attention of executives as a topic that needed further research.[32] It had always been there since Elliott Jaques had been using it in his publication *The Changing Culture of a Factory* (1951). But like most new discoveries, what emerged already existed except by name. One significant observation in this emergence was that culture in an organization must adapt to greater changes in society.[33] To that end, shared values came into the forefront acting like communication devices to manage culture.

> Company logos on employee's clothing became a dominant feature in the 1980s in attempts to create a homogenous community and abiding loyalty as a virtue of healthy society.

Company logos on employee's clothing became a dominant feature in the 1980s in attempts to create a homogenous commu-

---

[32] T. J. Peters and R. H. Waterman, *In Search of Excellence*, Harper and Row, 1982; T. E. Deal and R. A Kennedy, Corporate Cultures, Addison-Wesley, 1982.

[33] R. H. Kilmann, *Five Steps to Close the Culture Gap*. In R. H. Kilmann, M. Saxton, and R. Serpa and Associates (Eds) Gaining Control of the Corporate Culture, Jossey Bass, 1985.

nity and abiding loyalty as a virtue of healthy society.[34] This was quickly followed by encouraging stories of success or wins among employees where it was believed vital lessons could be learned as a unique combination of facts and sentiment. Executives took the risk of letting their managers express their own charisma to motivate their teams, much like a sports coach. Cheers and applause could be heard in the middle of the day recognizing someone's success on a particular team, but mostly in sales teams. So, the 1980s created heroes—even legends—in the workforce, but with it came far more losers.

Countering the win-lose scenario, W. G. Ouchi developed the idea of "Theory Z" by comparing what executives said their organization "should be" and "what it actual was" in the eyes of employees.[35] Reviving Chapple's idea from the 1940s that an organization was a living organism, Ouchi applied his ideas differently. For example, a living organism did not need the disruption of cheering and applauding, but coordination to succeed in developing a clear culture where everyone could flourish, not just the salespeople. His theory would only succeed if executives highly valued all their employees bringing out the best in everyone. As before in the 1940s, it may sound a little utopian, but Theory Z dealt with the balance of the long-term welfare of employees and then short-term profits, not the other way around.[36]

The need for balance between employee welfare and corporate profits was highlighted in the popular publication of *Corporate Cultures*.[37] Of the eighty organizations that were studied, only twenty-five had clearly articulated core beliefs. Of that group, only eighteen had qualitative beliefs and values, while the other seven had financially oriented goals. Upon further investigation, the organizations with qualitative beliefs and values outperformed all

---

[34] J. Martin, *Cultures and Organizations: Three Perspectives*, Oxford University Press, 1992.

[35] W. G. Ouchi, *Theory Z*. Addison-Wesley, 1981, 102.

[36] Ibid., 222.

[37] T. E. Deal and A. A. Kennedy, *Corporate Cultures*, Addison-Wesley, 1982.

other companies.[38] Remember, qualitative values deal with people, whereas quantitative values deal with the numbers produced by those people. A big discovery in the 1980s was that developing people ultimately impacted the bottom line.

The investigation also showed that 90 percent of what goes on in an organization had little to do with formal events, rather an informal hierarchy of "storytellers, whisperers, spies, and cabals" formed the cultural network for communication.[39] Four tribes, or clans, were identified as functional networks that facilitated this communication:[40]

> an informal hierarchy of "storytellers, whisperers, spies, and cabals" formed the cultural network for communication.

1. Tough guy, macho culture
2. The bet-your-company culture
3. The process culture
4. Work hard and play hard culture.

What these four tribes reveal is the importance of the business-social dynamic. I know it may sound ridiculous to reference but think about Brett Ellis' *American Psycho* (1991). No one is quite sure what Patrick Bateman did for a living, but his social connections were part of his promotion and apparent success. I must also mention the social side of his life also contributed to his psychotic breakdown.

Another aspect worth mentioning from the 1980s is the caution given to incoming executives not to realign corporate values with their own personal values. Corporate values become "corporate" because they often have heroes attached to them.[41] Such caution increased the need for independent consultants to work with

---

[38] Ibid., 14.

[39] T. E. Deal and A. A. Kennedy, *Corporate Cultures*, Addison-Wesley, 1982, 85.

[40] T. E. Deal and A. A. Kennedy, *Corporate Cultures*, Addison-Wesley, 1982, 107–108.

[41] Ibid., 158.

new executives to help them settle into their new role. Consultants also used various models to analyze the effectiveness of values. A popular model was called the *McKinsey S-7 Framework* where strategy, structure, systems, skills, staff, and style surrounded core values.[42] The seven dimensions could be meddled with by the new executive, but the core values were sacred. In *American Psycho*, Ellis deliberately made a point of portraying Patrick Bateman as a young executive who would not mess with corporate values. Also, think about the battles between IBM and Microsoft in the 1980s to get a better grasp of sacred values and variable practices.

Fight Club of the 1990s

The four tribes of the 1980s quickly morphed in the 1990s, changing the perspective of the business-social dynamic:[43]

1. Collaborative orientation
2. Adhocracy and creative orientation
3. Hierarchy with control orientation
4. Competitive orientation.

What these adapted tribes show is for executives to be effective, subcultures had to be engaged for the good for the organization.[44] Once again, we see the congruence of subcultures within organizational culture serving as vehicles for greater effectiveness. It may sound odd, but Chuck Palahniuk's[45] *Fight Club* (1996) epitomizes subculture. Though it would be counterproductive to have physical fighting in any organization, Palahniuk raises the awareness of what lies beneath the surface. We also see the same emphasis on executives as key players to the success of organizational culture. What we see much less of is the class system.

---

[42] T. J. Peters and R. H. Waterman Jr., *In Search of Excellence*, Harper and Row, 1982, 8–11.

[43] K. S. Cameron, R. E. Quinn, J. Degraff, and A. V. Thakor, *Competing Values Leadership*, Edward Elgar, 2006.

[44] Ibid., 2006, 160.

[45] Chuck Palahniuk, *Fight Club*, W. W. Norton, 1996.

To help executives, consultants introduced the idea of a "team culture" where access to information was broadened with more delegation through the vehicles of subculture.[46] This gave way to less control and more self-governance on certain levels of decision-making.[47] Once again, we see a further development of an organization like a living organism self-correcting itself functioning as a big family. The benefits of a team culture created the way for "customer service culture."[48] Others repackaged the idea of team culture focusing on a "marketing culture" or "sales culture."[49] For instance, if an employee had direct contact with a customer, it was also an opportunity to make a sales pitch whether an individual's job included a sale or not. In short, it was a culture of opportunity.

Summary

The second half of the 1900s stands in contrast to the first. Organizations no longer had a ruling class determined by their pedigree. Though blatant misogyny commenced the second half clocked by the world of snobbery and etiquette, by the 1990s the language of organizational culture had found a strong voice in research and practice. Lines of understandable communication were open from executives to their managers and the workers. What members experienced at work mattered more than ever. While the changes in the latter half of the 1900s are refreshing in comparison with today's world of organizational culture, a new tribe would enter the workforce: millennials.

Let's take a look at this highly popularized generation in the next chapter.

---

[46] E. Lawler, *Higher Involvement Management*, Jossey-Bass, 1968.

[47] C. E. Larson and F. M. J. Lafasto, *Teamwork*, Sage, 1986, 96–97.

[48] Maxine Melling and Joyce Little, *Building a Successful Customer Service Culture*, Facet Publishing, 2002, 143–205.

[49] M. Regini, J. Kitay and M. Baethge, *From Tellers to Sellers*, MIT Press, 1999.

CHAPTER FOUR

2000-2020S: FOREVER FLEXIBLE

After the world breathed a deep sigh of relief between December 31, 1999, and January 1, 2000, it was obvious that Y2K was not the start of an apocalypse and the rise of zombies. It was, however, the decade of millennials entering the workforce. It was a time of evolution and revolution in the way people worked together. Technology enhanced the business-social dynamic and how people interacted with each other. Coworking became popular by functioning in alternative spaces to a traditional office. Before the pandemic of 2020, people had already migrated to working from home or a coffee shop with internet access. Traditional attire was no longer proper etiquette—contrary to Amy Vanderbilt—and the cubical life gave way to open floor plans.

> It was, however, the decade of millennials entering the workforce.

Cloud Atlas in the 2000s

No one is quite sure of the connection, but open floor plans gave rise to models for organizational culture during the 2000s. A common model adapted in Britain and America had five components: [50]

---

[50]   Eric Flamholts, "Corporate Culture and the Bottom Line," *European Management Journal*, 19 (3), 268–275, 2001.

1. Treatment of customers
2. Treatment of people
3. Performance standards and accountability
4. Innovation and change
5. Process orientation

Other models would follow keeping to a similar pattern much like the threads that weave together David Mitchell's *Cloud Atlas* (2004). In the screenplay, Tom Hanks, Halle Berry, and Jim Broadbent took on multiple characters that spanned five centuries. Those characters were the thread that held it all together. People in organizations from the 1800s are still more or less the same people in the 2000s, but not quite. We have become far more aware of the cohesive power of culture in organizations and how it functions to hold things together.

Another advantage we have to our Dickensian predecessors is the language we use from the research about cultural organization. Cultural language was readily adapted in the 2000s and has changed our mood more than anything else. By mood, I don't mean moody, but a greater appreciation of all the members in an organization. In fact, the term "member" is now the motif for all positions in an organization prefixing executive, manager, director, president, supervisor, vice president, and more. The use of the word member has become widely used to describe a homogenous effort without the labeled clothing of the 1980s. In fact, the etiquette of the 1950s was practically disposed of in the early 2000s in terms of clothing and other aspects of personal presentation.

The Goon Squad in the 2010s

Remember, back in the 1920s researchers explored how a working environment impacted the productivity of people. Well, in this decade, bright and vibrant offices with a mix of different spaces to work evolved, bringing to life the concept of the "breakout space" where people wanted to spend time together to forge a deeper relationship with their brand and work culture.[51] Technology became

---

[51] https://www.condecosoftware.com/modern-workplace/history-of-the-workplace/#2010

exquisitely woven into the fabric of that workspace. People took more meetings by video conferencing or on interactive screens.

I think that Jennifer Egan's *A Visit from the Goon Squad* (2010) summarizes decades of development and comparison by highlighting the idiosyncrasies of seventeen characters from multiple generations with all their fads and trends. When organizational culture is viewed this way, we can only imagine what executives in the 1800s would have thought when members wanted more flexible work hours, where to work, and when to work. In my own imagination, I can hear characters like Mr. Bumble in Dickens' classic *Oliver Twist* (1838), "More!"[52] To which millennials would say, "Absolutely, what's wrong with that?"

> we can only imagine what executives in the 1800s would have thought when members wanted more flexible work hours, where to work, and when to work.

Agile working started to become a normal practice, and with that, hot-desking and flexible desk spaces. For the first time in the history of organizational culture, booking your desk time online was essential to productivity, something that Mr. Bumble could not possibly handle.

2020s Post-Pandemic

Another observation worth noting like an elephant in the room, so to speak, is the global pandemic of 2020. It displaced the workforce, and again by association, the displacement of customers and clients on an unprecedented scale. This time, people were forced to work away from the office and each other. It has brought to the surface questions that executives cannot delegate but must address directly at the highest level of an organization:

1. How do executives perceive people? Whatever is assumed about people will reflect in the way their members interact with each other and how those people are managed.

---

[52] Charles Dickens in Bentley's Miscellany Magazine (1837–1839), *Oliver Twist.*

2. In what way do executives define their organization and the members within it? Are they a family, team, group, partners, an association, and so on?
3. What metrics are executives using to know whether the members of their organization are doing well if they work from home or the office or a combination of both?
4. Do executives believe their culture is supported by the business strategy and organizational structure?
5. Does this relationship of strategy and structure enhance the day-to-day business of the organization?
6. What sentiment do executives encourage in the day-to-day business of the organization, and which emotions are discouraged?

We now live in a time where an old adage is center stage: is the glass half empty or half full? If we are in a post-pandemic time, some people will be left in a panic while others see the opportunity to re-imagine, re-invent, and re-think how the adhesive power of organizational culture can function to such a degree that people flourish and the bottom line is prosperous.

Summary

Questions are vital because "Anything that is measured and watched, improves."[53] Having read a very brief history of organizational culture in this section, I am sure you're already measuring the organization you represent and thinking of ways to improve it. So, I think it would be fair to say that today, "Employees who believe that management is concerned about them as a whole person—not just an employee—are more productive, more satisfied, and more fulfilled because satisfied employees mean satisfied customers, which leads to profitability."[54]

---

[53] Bob Parsons, founder of GoDaddy Group.

[54] Anne M. Mulcahy, CEO of Xerox.

Part One Conclusion

Most of what you've read in this first section—albeit a very brief account—is not found in typical history books. So, I think C. S. Lewis was accurate in his estimation about "the most important events." What we learn from the Dickensian world of the 1800s is a paternalistic approach to organizations from the small to extensive called company towns. Though exploitation and abuse were common, there were some hopeful historical moments where employers worked hard at the flourishing of people as well as profits. Interestingly, it is those small pockets of hope that have become significant priorities to executives today.

The first half of the 1900s taught us about the declining control of company towns and the importance of how people interpret their experiences at work. The ruling class, or higher class, dominated with the upper class wedged between them and the workers from the lower class of society. We also learn that very little research was conducted into how executives communicate with their managers and how workers understood things. What emerged was the sentiment of employees supported by unofficial channels called subcultures. Again, what seems remote and unimportant in the early 1900s is paramount in researching organizational culture today.

It was the second half of the 1900s that saw far more investigation into what organizational culture meant, how it functioned, and why it is important. Communication improved as the snobbery and etiquette of former decades ebbed to a manageable level. The 1980s were particularly educational in the sense that people began to talk officially and unofficially about the culture of organizations. Building on previous research, the importance of how members of an organization felt about their work experience began to take first place in most investigations. This naturally paved the way to a millennial generation entering the workplace driven by sentiment. I cannot

> Today, how we measure and improve organizational culture is high on the agendas of executives.

help thinking that the millennial generation was not self-created—as we often hear through social rhetoric—but a deliberate product of organizational culture from the 1990s.

Today, how we measure and improve organizational culture is high on the agendas of executives. The profitability of all the members in an organization is almost equal to financial profitability. Increasing salaries is not a guarantee that good people will stay with an organization anymore. And in the subsidence of a global pandemic, new and creative workspaces and ways of working have also come to the front of executive thinking.

I trust that you have found this brief history both useful and informative in your own understanding of how culture functions as an adhesive for everything in the organization you represent. As a culturist "who emphasizes the importance of culture in determining behavior and the way in which it functions," I hope you have also enjoyed the portraits I've tried to paint of cultural organization through popular literature, and even smiled at a few as you imagine people in your world as those characters. We all know a Scrooge, right?

I'm sure you are left with ideas emerging in your thinking. Write down in the space provided things that have come to mind about your own organization. When you arrive at the end of this book, I want you to come back to your first impressions here and see how those thoughts developed through each chapter.

So, what comes to mind?

_____

_____

_____

_____

_____

_____

_____

_____

_____

_____

_____

_____

In Part Two, I will lay out why organizational culture is your competitive advantage by defining what it means and why it is important in today's world, how to hire a great cultural fit, and how to keep good people by enabling them to become cultural adaptors.

PART TWO

ORGANIZATIONAL CULTURE IS YOUR COMPETITIVE ADVANTAGE

"Corporate culture is the only sustainable competitive advantage that is completely within the control of the entrepreneur."

(David Cummings, Cofounder of Patdot from his blog, *The Top Three Things Every Entrepreneur Should Know*, December 7, 2011)

This chapter will help you explore the opportunity to be in control of your sustainable competitive advantage through clearly understanding organizational culture, what it positively does for the members in your organization, and what it means to your competitors. In simple terms, your organization's competitive advantage answers this searching question: "What is it about our organization that affords us greater premiums in respect to our competition?"

Your organization's competitive advantage is confirmed when consumers[55] truly deem it unique and valuable—and therefore either pay a premium for your product or service and/or generate greater margins for the organization. This is precisely why people in the US will pay a premium for a cup of coffee from Starbucks and why people in Britain pay a premium to Costa Coffee. It has nothing to do with coffee itself. In 2019, there were about 1,000 Starbucks stores from which the company paid just £4m of tax to the exchequer despite raking in £387m in sales.

"Starbucks said it paid such a small amount of tax because it made a £17m pre-tax loss in the UK. The loss comes after paying out £75m in 'administrative expenses' which includes royalty payments of £27.4m. That means that Starbucks UK is paying about seven times more in royalty payments than it is paying in tax."[56]

It is perfectly legal and perfectly damaging to the culture of Starbucks in Britain where the British public perceive an American organization dodging their dues to the exchequer. Ironically, there is no Costa Coffee outlet in the US. In Chapter Five I quote Bob Parsons, the founder of GoDaddy, who talked about everyone watching and measuring organizational culture. Well, in this case, Starbucks was watch, measured, and boycotted, and put at a disadvantage in how the public viewed their culture. Admittedly, most of the British public probably did not bring pre-tax losses or royalty payments into their perception apart from a simple calculation: £387m in sales and only £4m in taxes. In my view, Starbucks lost their competitive advantage in the UK.

---

[55] Customers, clients, subscribers, donors, and attendee members.

[56] Rupert Neate for *The Guardian*, "Starbucks Pays £18.3m Tax but £348m in Dividends," June 27, 2019.

CHAPTER FIVE

WHAT DOES ORGANIZATIONAL CULTURE MEAN?

Definitions are useful when communicating something in any field. Definitions create clear thinking, which in turn help your members understand the culture of your organization. And you will see in the following chapters, unless a definition is clear, any organization is doomed to failure when looking for a cultural fit. Rather than stating a definition, I'd like you to think with me in this chapter and arrive at a dual effort.

Defining Organizational Culture

Most of the time organizational culture can mean completely different things from one person to the next because the idea of culture is a nebulous concept. It becomes difficult to explain or describe because it's use is generally ambiguous in organizations, much like the word love in relationships. For example, I can tell you that I love my dog and I love my children, but what I mean is different for both, right? Well, maybe when my children were going through their teenage years the dog was more favorable.

Ambiguity means organizations tend to lack a clear definition of what is meant by organizational culture. So, by the time someone is fired for not being a cultural fit, the person doing the firing and the person being fired really have no clear explanation of what just happened. Consequently, it does not help an organization, or the persons involved, to move forward. And let's not forget that it's a very costly business to let someone go for not being a cultural fit and then replace them.

A thriving organization is one with strongly held and widely shared values embedded in organizational culture. Though it is popular to assume human resources carry this responsibility, it is the executive leadership of an organization who create culture, as the members perpetuate it. New hires quickly come to understand and thrive in the culture of an organization through this intentional and perpetuating environment.

Instead of simply defining organizational culture as I see it, I'm going to ask a series of questions that will help you process a clear definition.

How does a thriving culture happen?

Current members already know how management wants them to respond in any given situation. Members also tend to believe this response as something good and healthy for them and the organization. Also, members know they will be recognized and rewarded for upholding the values of an organization.

Picture organizational culture like adhesive holding everything together.

Picture organizational culture like adhesive holding everything together. This adhesive focuses on how things get done rather than what gets done. So, culture can be referred to as the silent code of conduct, background aura, or white noise, yet it impacts everyone in the organization, especially new hires.

Organizational culture is not a product or service or something that an organization has to offer. Culture is what your organization is. A flourishing organization occurs when all members recognize that culture functions as an adhesive holding things together, and as such, shapes the relationships and behavior of every member on every level.

Where does organizational culture originate?

Though healthy organizational culture is perpetuated by its members, it originates with its executive leadership derived and exhibited from basic assumptions that lay the foundation for organizational culture. Remember during the 1800s and at least through the first half of the 1900s there was very little research in the relationship of executives and the rest of their members.

Whatever leaders assume about people will reflect in the way their members interact with each other and how those people are managed. So, does the executive leadership in your organization perceive people as inherently proactive or reactive, good or bad, hard working or lazy, mutable or immutable, trustable or untrusted, ethical or unethical? Write your answer in the space provided:

_____

_____

_____

The language that people use to describe the environment of your organization reveals how you are defined. So, does the executive leadership define its organization and the members within it as a family, team, group, partners, an association, and so on? Write your answer in the space provided:

_____

_____

_____

A thriving culture takes care of its people. So, describe the metrics the executive leadership uses that effectively measure how well its members are doing and whether they need further training to become better at what they do. Write your answer in the space provided:

_____

_____

_____

Typically, two options are in front of executive leadership in terms of strategy and structure in relationship to organization and culture. So, does the executive leadership believe the culture is supported by the business strategy or the organizational structure? Either option leads down very different paths. Write your answer in the space provided:

_____

_____

_____

All the members of your organization have emotions. If they didn't, they would not be human. So, does the executive leadership in your organization encourage certain emotions in day-to-day business? On the opposite end, which emotions are discouraged? If this is not done right, it can create fake people whose behavior and internal beliefs come into conflict. Write your answer in the space provided:

_____

_____

_____

Is organizational culture tangible or whimsical?

It is seen, felt, and heard in multiple ways. It evokes emotion. Some ways include corporate celebrations, internal and external communication, the behavior of its members, the use of images in marketing and promoting services and products, how and when individual members are recognized and rewarded, and much more.

> It is seen, felt, and heard in multiple ways.

Everything about the environment of an organization—the operating systems, procedures, tools, technology, policies, talent, and facilities—communicate organizational culture. In some cases, culture does not always relate to the official statements displayed on the wall or on the stationery. Organizational culture is more about what really matters to its members, how people really relate and work together, how everyone really experiences it, and how they make others feel.

So, what matters to your members? Write your answer in the space provided:

_____

_____

_____

Is organizational culture the same for everyone?

Organizations are not that different from each other. Everyone in an organization wants to optimize their positive reputation, productivity, and revenue, right? On one hand, these commonalities can be seen in organizations as dimensions of the whole. They include values, urgency, hierarchy, people and tasks, and sub-cultures. On the other hand, within those common dimensions are unique characteristics. Think about dimensions as building blocks and characteristics as the activities within those blocks. It's the activity within your organization that makes it unique.

Let's take a look at unique activity in four common dimensions. Read the brief description and answer the questions in the space provided:

Values: All organizations have values. Those values are not right or wrong, but each organization emphasizes the unique characteristics of its values.

1. In what way does your organization encourage ideas and experimentation with a degree of risk taking?

_____

_____

_____

2. To what degree is collaboration encouraged, celebrated, and rewarded?

_____

_____

_____

3. How focused are you on deadlines, achievements, and results?

_____

_____

_____

4. In what way does your organization pursue tolerance, fairness, respect, and acceptance of others?

_____

_____

_____

5. In what way is a healthy competitive spirit encouraged in your organization?

_____

_____

_____

6. How much attention to detail is given to approaching problem solving?

_____

_____

_____

Urgency: All organizations have a sense of urgency, whether it is intentional or not. Like values, a sense of urgency has unique dimensions to it, particular to your own organization.
1. Is the degree of urgency to which decisions are made driven by choice or forced upon your organization because of the movements in the marketplace?

_____

_____

_____

2. To what degree are projects and tasks pushed through quickly with a decisive management style?

_____

_____

_____

3. To what degree are projects and tasks moved forward at a reasonable pace with a curious management style?

_____

_____

_____

4. To what degree are projects and tasks moved forward slowly and consistently where the value of quality is preferred over efficiency?

_____

_____

_____

5. Does an indecisive culture prevail, and if so, why?

_____

_____

_____

Hierarchy: All organizations have forms of hierarchy whether you call each other by title, name, office, or something else.

1. Do the members of your organization work through official channels with precise job descriptions moving forward at a slow pace?

_____

_____

_____

2. Do members occasionally work outside official channels with general job descriptions moving forward at a quicker pace?

_____

_____

_____

3. Are members encouraged to challenge official channels with loose job descriptions moving forward at a fast pace?

_____

_____

_____

Alignment: All organizations are aggressive to some degree about valuing people and tasks. Some organizations choose their people to fit the tasks, whereas others must fit tasks to their operational process.

1. How oriented is your organization toward people when making decisions?

_____

_____

_____

2. In what way does the executive leadership demonstrate their understanding that people drive your organization in its productivity and performance?

_____

_____

_____

3. Does the executive leadership value tasks when making decisions, believing quality and efficiency drive your organization in its productivity and performance?

_____

_____

_____

4. Depending on the service or product of your organization, does the executive leadership emphasize a particular function that includes people and task orientation?

_____

_____

_____

What are the indicators of subcultures?

All organizations have varying subcultures unconsciously created by the traditions of individuals, previous practices, or geographical location where their members were raised as children. Subculture driven by individuals is unpredictable, as the nuances of tradition are personal to each member. At the end of the day, subcultures can help or hinder an organization.

Recognizing the key drivers in subcultures can help navigate them in a positive direction. Unconscious bias can simply come from the fact that people in organizations today are increasingly multicultural and multigenerational. This natural fact means that some members in an organization can be unaware of their behavior.

All organizations have varying subcultures unconsciously created by the traditions of individuals, previous practices, or geographical location where their members were raised as children.

1. How does your organization mitigate unconscious bias, if at all?

_____

_____

_____

2. Does your organization have a process for role modeling interculturally and cross-culturally with multicultural and multigenerational members?

_____

_____

_____

3. When conflicts arise—and we all know they do—there are many ways to bring resolution, but does your organization have methods of conflict resolution that address preexisting mindsets?

_____

_____

_____

4. To what degree is social intelligence implemented in your organization to address words and behaviors that have an impact on everyone? Higher levels of social intelligence tend to create higher levels of trust, whereas lower levels create the opposite.

_____

_____

_____

How is organizational culture managed?

To fully appreciate and understand the culture of any organization, cultural traits need to be identified. These traits are the activities that characterize day-to-day business. Typically, there are three types.

Ideological Culture: It is the sum of the beliefs, ideals, and values that members in your organization consider fundamental. If you are not aware of how this trait functions, listen to the words frequently used that shed light on intellectual and emotional interactions.

1. What intellectual words are frequently used?

_____

_____

_____

2. What emotional words are frequently used?

_____

_____

_____

Material Culture: Seen in how members work with and support each other. You can observe this support by noticing how resources are used with people in your organization that help and enhance each other's work. In short, a material culture is about collaboration.

1. In what way are resources used to enhance your work?

_____

_____

_____

2. In what way are resources used to help your work?

_____

_____

_____

Social Culture: Commonly called social culture amplified by what happens outside of work. Observing the roles and responsibilities of members in your organization outside of their job can be quite revealing. It can also be quite revealing how power is distributed in a social context to get something done at work. For example, the people who pull together a Christmas office party may be better at organizing it than management.

1. Do you participate with people from work in a social context? If so, why?

_____

_____

_____

2. Have you benefited from a social interaction with people you work with? If so, in what way?

_____

_____

_____

Summary

Organizational culture is like the adhesive that holds everything together. It originated with the executive leadership. Culture involves the sentiment of the members in how they feel about their experiences at work. Though most organizations have the same cultural dimensions, the activities within those dimensions differ from one organization to the other. Subcultures tend to promote or agitate the uniqueness of culture. However, organizational culture can be effectively managed.

Review your answers in this chapter and think about a definition for organizational culture. Is there anything about this definition you would disagree with? "The collection of values, expectations, and practices that guide and inform the actions of all members like a flexible adhesive." If you like this definition, great! If not, re-write your own definition in the space provided. Either way, remember how organizational culture is defined as you read through this book.

_____

_____

_____

Once you have a definition fixed in your thinking, let's look at what it means to be a cultural fit.

CHAPTER SIX

HIRING A CULTURAL FIT

Moe Carrick and Cammie Dunaway summed up the complexities of a cultural fit by writing, "It is largely invisible, unwritten and unspoken, but paradoxically, it causes employees the greatest pain, dissatisfaction, frustration and failure to thrive."[57] This chapter will help you toward hiring the right people, and when applied, it should relieve some of the pain, dissatisfaction, and frustration.

Clarity for a Cultural Fit

Have you said the following to one of your members, or have you been on the receiving end of someone telling you, "You're just not a good fit for the culture of our organization"? Members on the receiving

> "You're just not a good fit for the culture of our organization"

end of these fateful words are frequently left confused. Despite competence, experience, knowledge, and loyalty, something did not click with the executive leadership. The result: termination.

The same can be said for potential new hires who do their homework on an organization—becoming drawn to that organization's culture as a result—only to hear the fateful words at the

---

[57] Moe Carrick and Cammie Dunaway. *Fit Matters: How to Love Your Job*, Maven House, 2018, 43.

end of the interview or in a follow-up communication. The result: confused disappointment.

In the same fashion as the previous chapter, I'm going to ask a series of questions. Rather than giving you my opinion, I want to logically take you with me to see for yourself how important a cultural fit is to your organization.

When did a cultural fit become a thing?

The idea of a cultural fit emerged as a significant concept in the 1980s based on personality and values that connected with business strategy.[58] It was assumed that a cultural fit would make people feel more connected at work resulting in their desire to work hard, willingly embracing longer hours.

Over the past thirty years being a cultural fit has become a priority in hiring practices. In one recent survey, over 80 percent of employers said they would hire for culture and train for skill.[59] Today, the idea of being a cultural fit not only applies to potential new hires but extends to current members of an organization in their job performance, assessment, and evaluation. Consequently, being a cultural fit is something of an ongoing process that determines career success once hired by an organization. Answer the following two questions in the space provided about your organization:

1. How do your hiring practices include the idea of a cultural fit?

_____

_____

_____

---

[58] https://www.nytimes.com/2015/05/31/opinion/sunday/guess-who-doesnt-fit-in-at-work.html

[59] https://www.cubiks.com/insights/hire-culture-train-skill-recruiters-reject-candidates-based-their-lack-cultural-fit

2. How do your performance assessments and evaluations take into consideration the idea of a continued cultural fit?

_____

_____

_____

How is a cultural fit defined?

Though organizational culture tends to be nebulous in the way it is used, I described it in Chapter Five as the adhesive that holds everything together and defined as, "The collection of values, expectations, and practices that guide and inform the actions of all members like a flexible adhesive." Your organization's product or service, members, clients, customers, and various affiliates all come into contact with your culture. From this description and definition, your culture is not what your organization does, but how you do it, as evidenced in the behavior and practices of its members.

> your culture is not what your organization does, but how you do it, as evidenced in the behavior and practices of its members.

Consequently, the culture of your organization has a direct impact on its people, but equally true is the impact of people on the culture of your organization. The logical result of this dual impact is the focal point where each one intersects the other to decide whether someone is a cultural fit or not. Ideally, a member would be equally shaped by and contributing to organizational culture.

Figure 6.1 A Cultural Fit

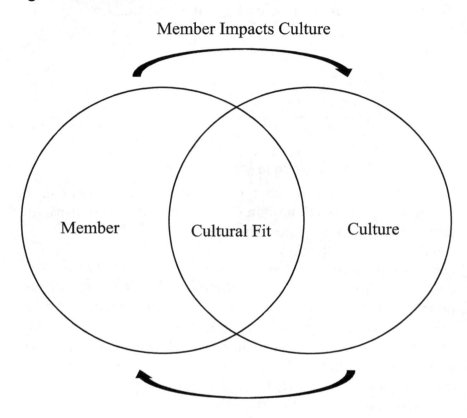

Let me ask you two questions about the members in your organization:

1. Are your people unsticking the adhesive that holds everything together, and if so, how?

_____

_____

_____

2. Are they strengthening the adhesive, and if so, how?

_____

_____

_____

Termination or promotion are the natural conclusions of each successive question when there is a clear understanding of organizational culture and how it works. However, this logical summary about being a cultural fit for current employees, and a fit for new hires, has recently become more façade that fact. Let me explain.

Are shared experiences really that important?

Circle back with me to the fateful statement that no one likes to hear or deliver, "You're just not a good fit for the culture of our organization."

When the gatekeepers of an organization look for people who they would enjoy socializing with, the idea of cultural fit becomes a façade in a "like-me-like-you" connection. Discovering shared experiences outside an organization during a job interview, or job performance, assessment, or evaluation are one thing, but discovering shared experiences on the job is quite something else. The latter results in strengthening the adhesive of organizational culture; the former does not and should not. Here's why.

Discovering an employee or potential new hire enjoys the same movies, books, sporting activities, and other recreational hobbies will make both parties feel warm and fuzzy, but is that the rise and fall of deciding whether someone is hired, fired, advanced, or promoted? At this point, a cultural fit becomes a per-

> When the gatekeepers of an organization look for people who they would enjoy socializing with, the idea of cultural fit becomes a façade in a "like-me-like-you" connection.

sonal fit. A personal fit revolves around a person, not the organization. It frequently ends in disaster because the professional boundaries often become friendship boundaries. Here are two questions to prompt your thinking. Answer in the space provided:

1. When was the last time you reviewed the questions that potential new hires are being asked in an interview?

_____

_____

_____

2. When was the last time you reviewed the performance evaluations and assessment questions of your current members?

_____

_____

_____

Figure 6.2 Appropriate Questions

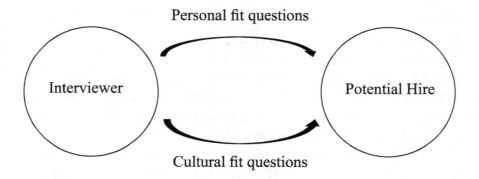

What is the ideal team?

When difficult and complex decisions are made, diversity on a team far outweighs people who are similar on the same team.[60] It is relatively easy to mistake a sense of rapport for expertise or skill, especially for a team involved in the hiring process. When a candidate is selected for hire or a current member is identified for promotion based on a personal fit, the demographic for unbiased diversity tends to plateau and even decrease. If this happens, quite often the team morphs into a new form of discrimination in the name of personal fit at the cost of cultural fit.

I have worked with great people and admire their skill, talent, ability, teamwork, passion, creativity, and much more. However, those people are not the only group I choose to socialize with outside of work. When we mesh the people in our lives comprised of professional networks, colleagues, associates, partners, and friends, we erase crucial boundary lines.

For example, the first four relationships I've listed above are largely transactional, whereas the latter—friendship—is something quite personal. I am not suggesting that one could not become the other. But I am suggesting that when warm and fuzzy become the epicenter of a cultural fit the ricochet effect lends itself to tit-for-tat issues that inevitably unstick the adhesive of culture that holds everything together.[61]

Here are two questions that will help you process this thought:

1. Who are the people on your team who do the hiring? List them.

_____

_____

_____

---

[60] https://insight.kellogg.northwestern.edu/article/better_decisions_through_diversity

[61] The infliction of an injury or insult in return for one that one has suffered.

2. Now look at that list and ask yourself if diversity is represented on the team. I am not just addressing ethnicity, gender, and age. More specifically, I am addressing the way people process information. If the list could change, write down your preferred team:

Current List   **Preferred List**

_____   _____

_____   _____

_____   _____

_____   _____

_____   _____

_____   _____

_____   _____

What needs to change?

One significant contributor to warm and fuzzy is the common practice of unstructured job interviews. I'll address this more directly in Chapter Eight. The same can be said for job performance assessments and evaluations. Are your people using tools for interpreting the results of an evaluation or assessment, or is interpretation left to the subjective feelings of the evaluator?

Figure 6.3 Interpreting Answers

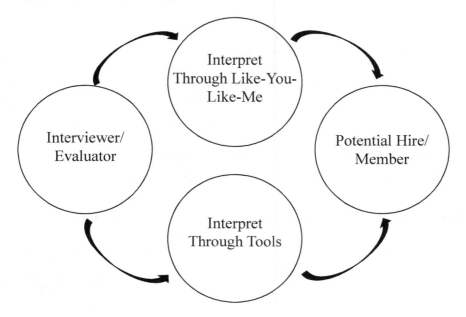

Without training interviewers and evaluators, a typical path that both find themselves walking on is that of connection rather than fit. Like watching a competitive TV show involving cooking, fashion, make-up, or design, and it comes down to three finalists, who do the judges choose? The one who they personally connect with.

Approaching potential new hires and current members—consciously or unconsciously—with a like-you-like-me attitude can become ripe for discrimination on who is hired, promoted, advanced, and fired in the name of a cultural fit. It can look like diversity, but left unchecked it has the potential to become an exclusive homogeny. The result: cultural chaos. Here's two more questions to help process this thought:

> Approaching potential new hires and current members—consciously or unconsciously—with a like-you-like-me attitude can become ripe for discrimination on who is hired, promoted, advanced, and fired in the name of a cultural fit.

1. How does your interviewing team interpret answers given by a potential new hire?

_____

_____

_____

2. How does your evaluating team interpret answers given by members of your organization in their performance reviews?

_____

_____

_____

Summary

The complexity of a cultural fit is known as invisible, unwritten, unspoken, and paradoxical. When a potential new hire and current member is not a good fit it can become the greatest pain, dissatisfaction, frustration, and failure to thrive. Nevertheless, when cultural fits are identified, it often results in the flourishing of an organization. Key processes need establishing that start with defining a cultural fit as opposed to personal fit. A great fit involves members who inform the culture as the culture informs the members. Interviewing processes need continued evaluation to avoid the like-you-like-me effect.

Now, review your answers to the questions in this chapter and ask yourself if pain, dissatisfaction, frustration, and failure to thrive is your current organizational experience. Though you cannot see it, read about it, or hear it, you know there is an imbalance in the culture of your organization. If so, it's time you reviewed what your people understand by a "cultural fit."

Now let's move on to specifically focus on your current members' cultural adaptors. Remember, it will typically cost your organization 150 percent of a current member's income if you replace them. So, think carefully through the next chapter on helping your people to adapt.

CHAPTER SEVEN

_____

KEEPING A CULTURAL ADAPTOR

Brian Halligan, CEO of Hubspot said, "The way I think about culture is that modern humans have radically changed the way that they work and the way that they live. Companies need to change the way they manage and lead to match the way that modern humans actually work and live." Whether he was conscious of it or not, Halligan echoes the sentiment of the 1930s where researchers took notice that changes in society directly impacted workplace behavior. In short, Halligan is talking about members of your organization culturally adapting.

I must add at this point that culturally adapting is not a one-shot wonder but an ongoing effort in response to the changes in society.

Adapting largely applies to current members who need to make shifts or changes to remain a cultural fit. It's where willingness to change and the capacity to learn and adjust go hand in hand. In a lesser way, culturally adapting also applies to new hires. Let me frame the context for cultural adaptors by quickly dealing with new hires.

Becoming a Cultural Adaptor

Potential new hires are less complicated in adapting to culture than current members. A new hire will enter an organization straight from college or from employment at another organization. That person can expect their onboarding to include an exhibition of a new culture through new people. However, a current member must adapt to a new culture largely with the same people and a steady stream of new hires. An exception may be when two organizations merge. Before I go any further, answer these two questions:

1. Did you find it easier to culturally adapt when you were first hired, or was it easier for you as your organization changed?

_____

_____

_____

2. Either way, did you adapt better on your own or with others in the same situation as you?

_____

_____

_____

All members in any organization must come to terms with the fact that change is essential to stay in business. Most would acknowledge the idea of change in operations, products, and services, but few take the time to recognize how this affects organizational culture.

When cultural changes are made it means members journey into uncharted territory. What lies ahead of an organization is not exactly like that organization's past. What current members understood in the past requires further understanding to succeed in the future. Also, the solutions to collaboration and problem-solving yesterday may not work tomorrow. The qualifications, education, and experience that got a member the job in the first place won't sustain them for the future. An adaptive capacity is essential.

> The first thing current members must do if they are to become cultural adaptors is learn to let go

The first thing current members must do if they are to become cultural adaptors is learn to let go—and in doing so—learn to close the gap between a developing culture and the present reality of the member. There are many strategies that can help, but for the sake of brevity, I'll present you five. Engaging these simple strategies can shorten the adjustment period and make it a smoother ride as a cultural adaptor:

Becoming curious

More than reading a memo, ask questions. Put some thought into how and when and to whom you ask questions. Curious questions will help you adapt to a developing organizational culture. Avoid critical questions because they may appear divisive and always flavor your conversation with appreciation to the person(s) you engage with. Write down three questions of curiosity that come to mind:

1. _____

2. _____

3. _____

Avoid being judgmental

Put effort into understanding your organization's developing culture by avoiding a judgmental attitude. A changing environment can appear strange, even wrong at first. But remember, you had no difficulty with adapting when your organization first hired you. When you understand the rationale for why things are done differently, it sheds light on issues you may have struggled with at work. Write down three things you have struggled with:

1. _____

2. _____

3. _____

Pause and reflect

Pausing and reflecting quite often prevents quick and rash conclusions. Certain behaviors that were acceptable may now be frowned upon. Pausing and reflecting helps you see things through the lens of a developing organizational cultural. Write down three things you are aware of that need to change about your behavior:

1. _____

2. _____

3. _____

Prepare for mistakes

Preparing yourself for mistakes is a healthy and humorous approach as you adapt to a changing culture. Most mistakes are subtle, so try to see the humorous side of things. The chances are that others will respond to you with support because you won't be the first to make a cultural faux pas. Have fun with this, and write down three mistakes that make you laugh or slightly embarrassed:

1. _____

2. _____

3. _____

Pursue support

Pursuing continued support of others is another healthy approach even if that means the help of someone who has only been with your organization a short time. Remember, they don't know the old organizational culture like you do so they are far less encumbered with it. Build cultural allies to clarify any confusion that you face. List your three best allies who can help you:

1. _____

2. _____

3. _____

The Art of Letting Go

New hires generally have ninety days to adapt to the culture of an organization. If current employees must let things go, new hires must quickly read the proverbial tea leaves of culture. There are differences for new hires straight from college, those who are hired from another organization, and those already working for an organization. The latter two are a mix of letting go of a previous culture, whereas the former has very little to let go. Either way, understanding organizational culture plays a big role in initial success.

> If current employees must let things go, new hires must quickly read the proverbial tea leaves of culture.

Again, there are many strategies that can help with letting go and understanding your organization adapting in its culture. Though the following suggestions are designed for current members adapting, they can easily be used for new hires.

Observe where and how

Observe where and how people collaborate, make decisions, and get things done that is different than your previous experience. It can save you a lot of frustration. How much time do people use meeting with one another? Do they work from home or from the office? Are your colleagues friendly and open to meeting with you? How many times do your colleagues cancel a meeting? Do you need others to help you make the necessary connections? Write down answers to these five questions:

1. _____

2. _____

3. _____

4. _____

5. _____

Notice how people communicate

Noticing how people communicate with each other teaches you the language of your organization. New hires will certainly add to the mix of communication. Do people go through formal channels in planned meetings where everyone is prepared? Is this accompanied by spontaneous communication with little documentation? The degree of hierarchy often determines whether you need to go through a personal assistant to communicate with someone. Are direct reports documented in a summary fashion with direct communication, or are you expected to detail those reports with a brief in-person meeting? Write down answers to these three questions:

1. _____

2. _____

3. _____

Watch the decision-making process

Taking note of the decision-making process will help you understand what methods people respond to and what they ignore. Are there informational meetings that result in informal decisions finalized by the executive leadership? When a decision is made, observe the process for implementing it. Is there a bias for action or a bias for more information? Either way, who are the stakeholders that influence the implementation of a decision? Write down answers to these three questions:

1. _____

2. _____

3. _____

Observe public recognition

Pay attention to the public recognition process in your organization. To what degree are people championed for their individual work and teamwork? The culture of your organization may accommodate problem-solving through collaboration, or it may lean toward individual innovation. Does your natural ambition emerge in a team or on your own? The key is to understand how the culture works. Write down answers to these two questions:

1. _____

2. _____

3. _____

Notice how people handle change

Look for how people handle change. You bring change to your organization by default as a new hire. Listen carefully to those around you and observe how people respond. You might be just the person they want to collaborate with, or not. If you were hired because your new employer noticed you are a change-agent, pace yourself with other employees. Buy-in to you, especially by new hires, is absolutely critical. Write down three reasons why you got the job:

1. _____

2. _____

3. _____

Summary

It is very rare for current members and new hires to become an immediate cultural fit with a natural capacity to learn and adjust. While both need to adapt, the dynamics are different. Engaging in simple and intentional strategies moves your organization away from cultural chaos and toward cultural conversion. Such a transition is inevitable in any organization because society has already changed the way we work and the way we live after the 2020 pandemic. We now manage, then lead this change to match the way we work and live.

Review your answers to the questions in this chapter and ask yourself if you are really adapting to a changing culture in your organization. Journal your observations from this chapter and commit them to memory as predictors of culture.

Part Two Conclusion

Having read through this section you will have a definition of organizational culture in mind. I like this one: "The collection of values, expectations, and practices that guide and inform the actions of all members like a flexible adhesive." You may have something different, but not by much. One of the key indicators of a vague culture is a lack of common consensus in what organizational culture means. Use the material in Chapter Five to help you become clear. Once you have arrived at a definition, make sure your team leaders use it as a thread that ties all discussions and decisions together. Defining what you mean is essential, especially when hiring.

The invisible, unwritten, unspoken, and paradoxical complexities of hiring a cultural fit have been and will always be challenging. There is no shortcut or escaping this phenomenon that will help or hinder the flourishing of your organization. On one hand, there is pain, dissatisfaction, frustration, and failure. On the other hand, there is tremendous momentum when cultural fits are identified, as the members inform culture as they are informed by the culture. This tension can cause interviewers and evaluators to take the shortcut while unconsciously looking for personal fits in the guise of cultural fit. I shall address this in more detail in the next section in Chapter Eight.

> In short, it will cost your organization 150 percent of the member's salary to replace them.

One aspect of identifying a cultural adaptor in your current members is for executives to observe who adds to the adhesiveness of culture, and who is dissolving it. The role of executives cannot be underestimated in terms of organizational culture. Though most organizations have the same cultural dimensions, the executives set the unique activities within those dimensions. This is the difference maker from one organization to another. So, arriving at a clear definition of organizational culture is a powerful motif for all members.

Another supposedly easy road to take is to fire a member and replace them. It may look like an easy road, but the cost is huge. In short, it will cost your organization 150 percent of the member's salary to replace them. Helping current members adapt to a changing culture can be emotionally expensive, but the long-term impact on successfully adapting is priceless. Overall, your organization must intentionally put a focused effort in hiring cultural fits and helping current members adapt. It has been my observation that a like-you-like-me approach has risen since the pandemic of 2020. Tools and methods are necessary to carry out intentions.

Like the previous section, I'm sure you are left with ideas that excite your thinking. Write down in the space provided things that have come to mind about your culture and how its powerful adhesiveness is seen in hiring cultural fits and developing cultural adaptors. Again, when you come to the end of this book, I want you to come back to your impressions of this section to see how those thoughts developed.

So, what comes to mind?

_____

_____

_____

_____

_____

_____

_____

_____

_____

_____

_____

The next section will take you through various measures to keep the culture of your organization current and effective with your members.

PART THREE

TAKING MEASURES FOR SUCCESS

"Leadership is a series of behaviors and measures rather than a role for heroes."

(Margaret Wheatle)

If you have traveled to London and taken the subway, you will be familiar with the announcement, "Mind the gap!" Passengers are cautioned to watch out for the space between the train and the platform. Not minding the gap can cause problems that inevitably hold everything up at the train station.

How members of an organization perceive their culture and what type of culture executive leadership needs to be successful can be viewed as the culture gap. Measuring that gap is a powerful indicator of whether organizational culture has buy-in from all its members.

It's no joke to say that "90% of employees within a winning company culture are confident in their company's leadership team."[62] I've said it in previous chapters and I'm going to

---

[62] Raine Digital. Online agency that works primarily with entrepreneurs, small to medium-sized businesses, startups, and non-profits, 2022.

say it again: organizational culture originates with the executive leaders. Other data tell us that 94 percent of executives and 88 percent of members say organizational culture is crucial to the company's success, and 90 percent of members who work in companies with a strong organizational culture are confident in the company's leadership.[63] In each case, the gap has been narrowed if not closed.

Even though the idea of culture is rather nebulous, I hope the previous chapters helped you gain a clear definition. Without this definition, closing the gap between executives and their members can be a futile task. But it's not just a matter of definition. Questions about the function of organizational culture as an adhesive to people and processes, fitting with it, and adapting to it must be asked and answered with clarity.

In this third section I will address interview techniques, performance indicators, and agility. All three can be measured to see if the gap is widening, staying the same, or closing. The latter is your goal.

---

[63] Greg Kihlstrom for *Forbes Magazine,* 2020.

CHAPTER EIGHT

MEASURING AN INTERVIEW PROCESS

Without a doubt, people are attracted to your organization before they apply. There is something about you they like. If so, I think it highlights what Jessica Herrin, the CEO and founder of Stella Dot, says: "Shaping your culture is more than half done when you hire your team." Your team showcases who you are as an organization. Shaping organizational culture is to shape your team that attracts applicants. Of all the reasons to develop organizational culture, this is a powerful one.

Measuring the Interview Process

In this chapter I will address nine practical steps that you can implement to measure an interview process. When candidates who are attracted to your organization make an application that leads to an interview, their cultural perception and your reality should complement each other. Let me defer again to Justin Mc-Leod, founder and CEO of Hinge, who points out what happens when the applicant does not understand your culture: "It's likely the person [you hire] becomes a drain rather than a contributor to the company – even the really smart, talented ones." So, as Herrin would have it, let's start with briefly analyzing your organizational culture to gain a little more clarity.

Quick Cultural Analysis

What you do as an organization is already understood by an applicant. But how do you do it? If you don't know the answer, I'm sure the candidate sitting in front of you has a good idea. You see, applicants do a great deal of research into the organization they are applying to. Admittedly, there are commonalities and differences in how executive leaders describe their organizational culture, and how the members describe it. You've read about that in previous chapters, and you will read about it in the next two. But let's face it, unless your organization is the collective mind of Borg from Star Trek,[64] the idea that everything being clear to everyone is a bit of a myth. However, there should be more commonalities than differences.

> But let's face it, unless your organization is the collective mind of Borg from Star Trek, the idea that everything being clear to everyone is a bit of a myth.

So, what motivates the members of your organization? Whatever the answer is, it should translate into the core competences of your business. For example, if you really do value teamwork, what makes your teams stand out? Again, I bet the candidate in front of you has a good idea. And I equally bet they have figured out how your business and culture are linked.

There is an ancient Greek aphorism called "know thyself" originally carved into the temple of Apollo at Delphi.[65] You will see its Latin translation in colleges and universities in the West *nosce te ipsum or temet nosce* as a reminder that we had better be sure about who we are. Over time, "know thyself" became "know thy measure."[66] Before the person being interviewed sat down in front

---

[64] The Borg are fictious cyborgs linked together in a hive mind called the Collective. The Borg forcibly assimilate everyone into the Collective.

[65] Greek writer Pausanias (10.24.1).

[66] Wilkins, Eliza G., *Classical Philology*, 1927, University of Chicago Press, 22 (2): 121–135.

of you, they measured your organization. It led to an application that led to an interview. Now, as someone interviewing the candidate, do you know the cultural measure of your organization?

Be honest with yourself and circle the answer that comes to mind:

1. Absolutely
2. Generally
3. Vaguely
4. Not at all

Unless you answered by circling the first option, do the work of getting to know who you are as an organization seen in the commonalities that align with executives and members.

Brand and culture

Organizational culture and brand are a two-way dynamic. Your culture is delivered through your brand, and your brand through your culture. Potential candidates will opt in or out beginning with this dynamic. You can deliver your culture on a website but it's not enough. Remember what Herrin said, "Shaping your culture is more than half done when you hire your team." Though a website is necessary, it not your team. Can people get a job tour of your organization —virtually or in person—to gain a better understanding of who you are? If so, who will they intentionally meet on that tour? If you are looking for the most qualified candidates, does qualification mean their experience or their cultural fit?

> Your culture is delivered through your brand, and your brand through your culture.

A great way of helping candidates opt in or opt out of applying for a job is to offer a self-test that measures if they are a good cultural fit. However, even if they are a fit, you will want to pursue their fit-ness in person using their results as a guide. Remember, some people are good at tests and others shine in face-to-face meetings.

Don't be put off if candidates don't apply or accept an offer. You still stand to benefit from the exercise. Remember the words of Justin McCleod in his comments about hiring the wrong person: "It's likely the person becomes a drain rather than a contributor to the company – even the really smart, talented ones."

So, in what way do you showcase the brand of your organizational culture for candidates to decide if they want to apply or not? Write your answer in the space provided:

_____

_____

_____

Develop behavioral based interviews

Structured interview procedures will help you determine if a candidate has the core competencies central to your organization's culture. There are multiple competencies that your organization cannot train people to have, like integrity, good judgment, honesty, reliability, and many more. There are other competencies that you don't care to train because you expect a candidate to already know them. A range of software applications may be an example. So, ask questions around behavioral competencies. But those questions need to drill down on reality.

What a candidate did in a previous job will give you a good indication on how they will behave in your organization. Ask them questions about their previous job by creating scenarios with open-ended answers. Create a dilemma, a problem, or a situation common in most organizations and look for their response.

Write down three questions that come to mind in the space provided:

1. _____

_____

_____

2. _____

_____

_____

3. _____

_____

_____

Validate your assessments

Be very sure that all your self-test assessments meet with current legal and professional standards. Do the assessment questions have some relationship to large turnover in your organization? The answer to this specific question cannot be arrived at immediately. It can take up to a year to get the data you need to track the answer. If the answer is yes, you may want to further validate your assessments. Either way, your assessments require attention and hard work.

Role-play

Get creative in how to set up role-play for a candidate. Perhaps get a team leader to role-play as a member of a team with complaints about their tasks. How is the potential new hire going to handle it? If it is feasible, put them in a live situation under observation to see how they handle themselves. If it involves sales or customer service, the options available to you are endless—and can be a lot of fun for you and the candidate. Much like the CBS show *Undercover Boss*, you can have front row seats to how candidates handle themselves.

Without using the ideas above, write down three role-play ideas that show you how a potential new hire conducts himself or herself:

1. _____

_____

_____

2. _____

_____

_____

3. _____

_____

_____

Legalities and the Law

Any process you have that measures a candidate's potential hire that has the effect of excluding and discriminating is an absolute no. Get it out of your thinking the general idea that you can hire people based on nonjob-related reasons so long as you're not intentionally discriminating. Nonjob-related reasons can be highly discriminating. It sometimes occurs—not because of something intentional—but because elements of the application, interviewing, and hiring process produced discriminatory outcomes.

> Get it out of your thinking the general idea that you can hire people based on nonjob-related reasons so long as you're not intentionally discriminating.

Think about validating all your assessments reflecting on the previous section above. If, after a year of collecting data, you discover that information suggests bias, there could be systemic discrimination without you consciously being aware of it. Data is therefore king!

When organizations purchase tests from third-party vendors, they do so with assurances that the tools they are buying have already been validated against discrimination. "That means there is sufficient evidence to confirm that people in protected categories who take the test will not be adversely affected in the scoring. In most instances, that appears to be good enough."[67]

Be Meaningful

Keep to some simple math: separate cultural fit data from your cost-per-hire, time-to-fill, and quality-of-hire statistics, and then monitor culture regularly. What percentage of entry-level positions do you want filled over the next twelve months? And how many non-entry-level positions do you want filling over the same period of time?

Whatever these percentages are, what does it tell you about selecting the right people? Write your answer in the space provided:

_____

_____

_____

Train your interviewers

Train your people in behavioral interviewing techniques that ask intelligent questions, including follow-up questions, with the goal of arriving at a clear picture of the candidate. I mentioned in Chapter Six the idea of a cultural fit has somehow morphed into a personal fit of like-you-like-me. Now, if you are developing a book club outside of your organization, go ahead but don't discriminate. Avoid the trap of personal fit in the guise of a cultural fit.

---

[67] SHRM, 2020.

What training, if any, does your organization offer to train interviewers? Write your answer in the space provided:

_____

_____

_____

Keep a paper trail

There are three big costs to life in the West: education, medication, and litigation. It is the latter that concerns us here. If your organization is audited under suspicion of discrimination, an excellent paper trail will substantiate your position. By "paper trail" I mean electronic records. There are people in the world who have a natural ability to compile information like this in an accessible way. Much like the mind palace of Sir Arthur Conan Doyle's fictitious character, *Sherlock Holmes*. Remember that data is much like Switzerland, it is neutral until it is applied. Hire people who love collecting, analyzing, and making data accessible, but make sure the hiring process is not discriminatory.

> Remember that data is much like Switzerland, it is neutral until it is applied.

Summary

People are attracted to your organization before they make an application, so "Shaping your culture is more than half done when you hire your team." Hiring the right people is challenging when candidates have done considerable research about your organization. You don't want the candidate to know more about you than you do the candidate. And you don't want to discriminate through bias. Measuring your process from application to interview to hire will help you. Review the answer to the questions in this chapter and make note of anything missing in your organization.

In the next chapter I will take it further than measuring interviewing processes. If it is true that everything can be measured, let's look at how you can accomplish this task.

CHAPTER NINE

MEASURING CULTURAL PERFORMANCE INDICATORS

In Chapter One, I quoted Bob Parsons, the founder of GoDaddy, who said "Anything that is measured and watched, improves." But who is watching and measuring? The answer is everyone. Executives, members, clients, and anyone else in contact with your organization. I think David Mattin from TrendWatching accurately summarized the "everyone" answer when he said, "People can see all the way inside. Every person. Every process. Every value. Everything that happens, ever. There's a single word that sums up what a person sees when they look deep inside your business: they see your culture."[68]

> Key performance indicators can be measured by looking at cross-departmental collaboration and the frequency of feedback provided by teams.

If everyone is watching, in all probability, any measuring taking place is not a valid method but more of a personal perception. It's how they feel about what they observe. While perception is valid in several ways, it's not as comprehensive as you think. Your organization can develop valid and reliable methods for measur-

---

[68] David Mattin, Head of Trends & Insights at TrendWatching, 2020.

ing what is observed. This chapter will deal with methods for measuring the culture of your organization.

Key Performance Indicators

Key performance indicators can be measured by looking at cross-departmental collaboration and the frequency of feedback provided by teams—not just within a team—but with other teams in your organization. While a competitive spirit can be healthy, it should not be at the cost of collaboration with other teams. These indicators help executives to draw conclusions on how well aligned their culture is in terms of accountability. Here are six checks and balances that are useful to executives on measuring accountability. Let's look at them in the form of questions.

Are priorities clear?

We've all worked hard on a project only to discover that priorities have shifted. After adjusting ourselves, we find priorities have shifted again. These shifts leave a wake of frustration on what the organization is trying to achieve. A good method that reduces frustration is to limit objectives to a handful of significant goals clearly articulated as a standard of accountability. Used in all teams, it can be very effective.

What are the three meaningful and memorable goals your organization is trying to achieve right now? Write your answers in the space provided:

1. _____

_____

_____

2. _____

_____

_____

3. _____

_____

_____

Members of any organization should know these big goals at the drop of a hat. As such, all priorities orbit around these goals. All initiatives and results framed within this orbit only work when everyone has a good grasp on them.

What is the morale of your members?

Inadequate and unclear communication is usually a result of poor accountability that negatively impacts morale. You know exactly what I am talking about here. How do members of a team know if they are making a difference or not? Well, there is nothing like feedback because people feel heard, respected, and inspired when others listen. Ask yourself these two questions and write your answers down in the space provided:

In what way and how frequently does leadership check in with the members of your organization?

1. _____

_____

_____

In what way do you think feedback can become an inspirational method in your organization?

2. _____

_____

_____

What are the trust levels?

Brian Chesky, the cofounder and CEO of the highly successful Airbnb said, "When the culture is strong, you can trust everyone to do the right thing."[69] Trust is a premium in any organization. So, if you measured the trust levels, what would the results look like? There is nothing worse than when distrust is spread throughout your organization. Colleagues inevitably become defensive and ultimately counterproductive to problem solving through collaboration.

> Trust is a premium in any organization.

There are multiple reasons for a loss of trust. A loss of trust typically deals a lapse in accountability. Promises are made but not delivered. Fostering healthy accountability around the three to four main things your organization is trying to achieve produces high levels of trust.

Ask yourself the following two questions and write your answers down in the space provided:

1. What are some behaviors that have created a lack of trust in your organization?

_____

_____

_____

2. What are the behaviors that foster trust in your organization?

_____

_____

_____

[69] Brian Chesky, cofounder and CEO, Airbnb, 2020.

Is there declining engagement?

Like morale, a noticeable decline in engagement typically looks like members disconnecting from their team and a decline in collaborating with other teams. A lack of personal investment means leadership must address a sense of purpose.

What lurks at the heart of declining engagement is a lack of daily connection. A word of encouragement, constructive feedback, and momentary recognition for problem solving all help members of your organization understand the measurable ways their individual work has a real impact.

Reflect on these three questions as your write down your answers:

1. When was the last time you encouraged someone in their work, and who was it? Why did you feel the need to encourage this person?

_____

_____

_____

2. What response did you receive from this person, and how did you feel about offering your own encouragement?

_____

_____

_____

3. When was the last time you were encouraged by a member of your organization, how were you encouraged, and why do you think that person encouraged you?

_____

_____

_____

_____

Is there ineffective delivery?

Your schedule can be filled with meetings that can seem to run back-to-back. Whether those meetings are one-on-one, team oriented, or high level in the organization, if you are not achieving the objectives of these meetings, again, there is probably a lack of accountability.

It can be mentally defeating to see a seemingly impassable crevice open between a goal and the actual outcome of hard work. If a bridge can be built over this crevice, there are two key things that will anchor that keep it accountable: people and process. Both need a radical re-imaging of reality. To be accountable is to bring together responsibility and reality.

Being reactive, impulsive, reckless, or punitive will never bring a team together. Think about a sports coach you admire who just lost a game. Your admiration does not stem from the loss but from the fact the coach held himself responsible for his team. I remember admiring Gareth Southgate who took the English soccer team to the final game of the 2020 European Cup. England lost to Italy on penalties, but Southgate took full responsibility. The British people loved him **for it.**

Building the bridge with people and process is to say three definitive and timely things:

1. We've made a great start!
2. We're already halfway there!
3. We've made it!

You can add at least two more positive affirmations that break the whole process down into quarters. In fact, try that out by writing your own four statements here:

1. _____!

2. _____!

3. _____!

4. _____!

Become known as the organizational member who people love to be around, no matter your position in your organization.

Is there a large turnover?

I have worked for several organizations where the turnover of members was extraordinarily high. One was a prestigious university and the other a very large church. I am convinced that in both cases the culture of the organization was vague and known only to a few. But most of all, when leaders talked about culture, it changed from month to month. At such a pace, no one could culturally adapt.

People grow tired at work, and I am not talking about physical or mental tiredness. The kind of weariness that sets in goes to the heart of a member where Monday morning is a loathsome task and Friday afternoon is a tonic relief. Most of the time, tiredness like this stems from unclear expectations creating a tension between leadership and its members, widening the cultural gap.

There is a line in any organization—as there is in your organization—that marks the point of tiredness as I've described it.

> Ultimately, people leave your organization because they have grown tired of not accomplishing anything measurable at work.

Working above the line assumes personal responsibility, clear expectations, achievable results, and the action to achieve this. Below the line assumes blame, unqualified excuses, and a lack of motivation. Once the members of your organization fall below the line, it can be like raising the Titanic. Ultimately, people leave your organization because they have grown tired of not accomplishing anything measurable at work. So be proactive about your people.

Figure 9.1 The Organizational Line

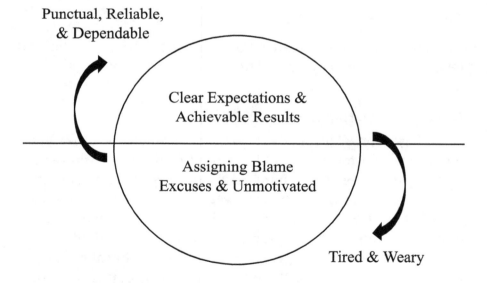

Punctual, Reliable, & Dependable

Clear Expectations & Achievable Results

Assigning Blame Excuses & Unmotivated

Tired & Weary

While I have mentioned a few noticeable characteristics about people who drop below the line, in what way can you measure the line? What's above it and what's below it? Think about the illustration above and draw your own.

1. Draw a line across a piece of blank paper.
2. Write above the line ascending characteristics. For example, content, happy, enthused, energetic, ambitious, and so on.
3. Write below the line descending characteristics. For example, discontent, unhappy, unenthusiastic, no energy, no ambition, and so on.

Using this simple diagram, answer the following two questions:
1. In what way can leadership engage its members to sustain the culture of your organization?

_____

_____

_____

2. In what way can leadership engage its members to grow the culture of your organization?

_____

_____

_____

If your organizational culture is unclear, vague, known only to a few, and changing too fast for members to adapt, think about how you have answered the two questions above. It may be within your scope to raise the Titanic!

Summary

Everything about your organization can be measured and watched and be improved. Everyone is watching and can see all the way inside to every person, process, and value. People see your culture. Key performance indicators that can intentionally track your culture and stop the hemorrhaging of good people leaving range from checking priorities, developing trust levels, increasing the morale of your members, displaying effective engagement, and having timely delivery. Review your answers to the questions in this chapter and ask yourself if there is anything you can do right now to implement the performance indicators above.

Now that you have thought about measuring culture through performance indicators, let's take a look at measuring the agility of your organization.

CHAPTER TEN

MEASURING ORGANIZATIONAL AGILITY

Agility is all about taking the pulse of your organization by measuring the rate of adaptability, goals accomplished, achievements, and degree of member engagement. Though executives can measure these four aspects of agility, they cannot control the market environment that can cause your organizational pulse to race a little, or a lot. What they can control is the "corporate culture as the only sustainable competitive advantage completely within the control of leadership."[70]

> So, agility is your organization's ability to measure what needs to calm down and what needs to pick the pace up.

So, agility is your organization's ability to measure what needs to calm down and what needs to pick the pace up. Let's look briefly at the four aspects that give us the pulse of an organization and ask some probing questions about your role in your organization:

---

[70] David Cummings, cofounder of Pardot, 2011.

Rate of Adaptability

As a common rule of thumb, there are six major forces driving organizational culture toward adapting. All six may not receive the same consideration in your organization, but I guarantee a combination of at least four will draw your attention.

Commoditization

How did Walmart manage to surpass Sears as the number one retailer in 1992? Walmart simply out-innovated Sears in the cost of goods, cost of distribution, and pricing. In short, commoditization typically drives costs down by innovative outsourcing. In 2022, we can say the same thing about Uber out-innovating traditional taxi cabs, Airbnb typical accommodation, Fandom the gaming world, Clockify traditional schedule keeping, and many more.

So, how is your organization deploying innovation in response to commoditization? If you are unsure, then you'll not be able to measure it. Write your answer in the space provided:

_____

_____

_____

Technology

The second force could be called the digital world. IBM was certainly not agile enough when Arvind Krishna CEO restructured the organization by cutting 200,000 jobs.[71] Technology no longer belongs to the giant corporations. It's readily available to startups and small organizations that have a domino effect on operational costs and increased IT capabilities.

Nevertheless, giants like Home Depot have taken huge steps incorporating technology in the sale of construction and home

---

[71] Jessica Bursztynsky, CNBC, May 22, 2020.

improvement materials and design.[72] Technology is now used by farmers who plow, treat their land, and harvest from information delivered by satellites. In fact, all of society is impacted by digitalization not only in business, but also in entertainment, recreation, education, and even the arts. Agility through technology is everywhere.

In what way has the digital world impacted your organization in the past three years, and at what rate is it growing? Write your answer in the space provided:

_____

_____

_____

_____

Social Media

The impact of social media throughout society is an absolute cultural norm. When digital technology is progressively applied in day-to-day living, its function is directed to all of society. It is impossible to be in business today without the internet—even with farmers—and the endless software tools and updates to manage operations. This pervading use is of enormous importance when an organization is adapting.

> This pervading use is of enormous importance when an organization is adapting.

---

[72] Retail Information Systems, July 23, 2021.

How is the use of prevalent social media affecting your organization? Write your answer in the space provided:

_____

_____

_____

Glocalization

The phenomena of glocalization was popularized when the internet became popular from about 1989. Essentially, local and global become a single market or community. Economic systems added to social media means invited participation in a singular system. People in your organization are participating in social and business communities from other countries. They are transcending national boundaries.

Local business must now be aware of global trends to understand how operations can be impacted by the decisions of others on the other side of the world. Therefore, adapting means optimizing learning opportunities by intentionally interacting with communities in other communities beyond national borders.

In what way does your organization function in a glocal world? Write your answer in the space provided:

_____

_____

_____

Tumultuous World

Some may say the world has always been tumultuous. Turn on the news on any day at any time on any channel. You will hear reports that could be categorized as "trouble of every kind." It's enough to remind us that the world we live in is in constant turmoil. On one hand, someone is sophistically threatening someone else in the political arena, while on the other hand the same thing occurs in the streets of your community with far less sophistication. Someone is racist, homophobic, xenophobic, misogynist, offensive, politically incorrect, and so on. As tradition goes, the news concludes with a humorous story in attempts to distract us from a tumultuous world. But are we that fickle?

How does your organization anticipate turbulence, and how does it typically respond? Write your answer in the space provided:

_____

_____

_____

Increased speed at the same pace

The final force that makes the organizational pulse race is increased speed to stay in the same place. The previous five forces are strategic issues central to your organization's planning. But each force does not occur independently of each other. Rather, they are mutually interdependent, feeding off one another. As the collective impact converges, unavoidable acceleration takes place, and as a result, the inescapable amplification of their impact is made evident.

> The final force that makes the organizational pulse race is increased speed to stay in the same place.

So, developing a strategic response to capture the power of innovation is not only a necessity but a marvelous opportunity that should not be ignored.

How is your organization harnessing innovation as you pick up speed at the same pace? Write your answer in the space provided:

_____

_____

_____

Rate of Goals Accomplished

The second aspect that will give you the pulse rate of your organization is all about celebrating goals. Office parties, casual Fridays, or a happy hour can become part of celebrating goals accomplished. It creates a moment of positivity and pause to realize the importance of what lies at the heart of organizational culture. The story of Bristol Farms will help to illustrate this.

Bristol Farms had a series of buyouts in 2014 as the members struggled with dissatisfaction and burnout. There was no evidence that their long-term goals were linked in any way to their short-term goals. So, they did something remarkable by working hard at developing a common language for all members. This was their link. It not only transformed their unproductive culture of sarcasm to a culture of positive, collaborative, solutions-oriented communication, it set a long-term plan that everyone could articulate in their day-to-day work. There are two things we learn from this:

Great communication unlocks member engagement

Bristol Farms accomplished a 7.7 percent growth in year-over-year sales and increased product sales by 22 percent in an otherwise stagnant industry. Developing a common language helped all the members renew their commitment to organizational culture. Better lines of communication and cross-functional accountability flourished. Instead of viewing communication and feedback as a one-way street, it created a dynamic and egalitarian openness across organizational levels with a positive effect on member attitudes.

When all members of your organization feel comfortable giving feedback to and from their coworkers and superiors, the result is nothing short of a culture of trust and increased accountability. Feedback loops tend to inspire increased accountability defined as "a personal choice to rise above one's circumstances and demonstrate the ownership necessary for achieving desired results."[73] This is always good news for an organization.

> Feedback loops tend to inspire increased accountability

Write down in the space provided three to four words that describe the common language of your organization, whether they are positive or negative.

_____

_____

_____

Positive culture creates profitability

The second thing we learn is that to never underestimate the powerful relationship of a positive culture and profitability as the financial bottom line and the well-being of your members. Better business results will always follow highly motivated people. And profitability done well should increase the income of all members.

It really should come as no surprise that happy members are more productive. Think about this in terms of increased speed at the same pace I mentioned earlier in this chapter. If you want to be factual (and why not?), when members feel positive about their work, 85% take more initiative, 73% tend to be more collaborative, and 48% care more about the results of their work.[74]

---

[73] Craig Hickman, Tony Smith, and Roger Connors, *The Oz Principle*, Portfolio, 2010.

[74] Culture Partners, *Improving Employee Satisfaction Through Positive Accountability*, 2020.

In what way would you describe the current relationship of organizational culture and profitability? Write your answer in the space provided:

_____

_____

_____

Rate of Achievements

The third aspect with respect to the pulse rate of your organization is about achievements. While goals certainly point to delivering results, *achievement* highlights the method of accomplishing those goals. As such, *the rate* of achievement occurring at every level of an organization is important, yet frequently ignored or misunderstood.

There are many terms for process-related management tools that speak to flexibility, pace, and togetherness. However, those terms are used generally in IT teams. I want to suggest two significant ways of cultivating achievement, as I defined it, across all members of your organization.

Aligning members around shared objectives

Often, an individual member has a personal set of daily priorities to achieve goals that do not always align with team goals, or even the objectives of a given project being worked on by that member and their team. Also, the team's goals may not support the larger vision of the organization in the three or four things it is trying to accomplish. In reality, no individual member or team can accomplish a high level of achievement unless there is clarity on what the organization is aiming for. Therefore, achievement in the workplace must begin with aligning a clear set of objectives with the organization's goals.

Who is responsible for this clarity? Simply put, executive leadership. They make it clear what the three to four things the organization is wanting to accomplish within a specified period. This kind of clarity defines what the results look like. They are measurable, meaningful, and memorable.

In the space provided, paint the picture of what the objectives look like. If you are not clear, say so.

_____

_____

_____

_____

Fostering achievement through accountability

The second way of cultivating achievement is a strong sense of alignment with individual members through accountability. Without accountability, alignment fails. Remember, responsibility must not be confused with accountability. The first is all about ownership in the roles and duties of a task, whereas the latter tends to be accompanied with the question, "What else can I do?" Viewed this way, accountability is about doing whatever it takes to complete the task.

> Without accountability, alignment fails.

Remember, accountability is the "personal choice to rise above one's circumstances and demonstrate the ownership necessary for achieving desired results."[75] This kind of accountability not only requires members and teams to take ownership of their role and function in a task but have a daily commitment to problem solve through collaboration, overcoming setbacks and obstacles that inevitably present themselves throughout the process of getting something done. Consequently, achievement can be self-perpetuating in an accountable culture. It's where mem-

---

[75] Craig Hickman, Tony Smith, and Roger Connors, *The Oz Principle*, Portfolio, 2010, 190.

bers hold themselves accountable and responsible for high personal achievement.

Separate your responsibility and being held accountable. Now answer the following two questions in the space provided:

1. What daily steps do you take to ensure responsibility for the tasks given to you?

_____

_____

_____

2. What daily steps do you take to ensure accountability for the tasks given to you?

_____

_____

_____

Rate of Member Engagement

The third aspect of checking the pulse rate of your organization is about member engagement. Now, I don't want to sound oversimplified, but how is member engagement defined? It is a personal commitment to your organization and the achievement of its objectives. Surprisingly, after the global pandemic of 2020, member engagement increased to 39% in January 2021, up from 36% late last year.[76] Fostering this momentum is more important than ever because it positively impacts organizational success. It can be measured and promoted. Let's look at two realities of member engagement.

---

[76] Gallup Poll, *U.S. Employee Engagement Rises Following Wild 2020*, February 26, 2021.

It's critical to the success of your organization

The first reality is when members are actively engaged in their work and committed to meeting goals. As such, it is highly probable they will proactively identify problems, take ownership for problem solving, and offer solutions. As a result, organizations with highly engaged members are proven to outperform competitors upwards of 145% of total earnings per share.[77]

> organizations with highly engaged members are proven to outperform competitors upwards of 145% of total earnings per share.

However, the opposite is also true. Disengagement is often a result of low job satisfaction, a loss of trust, unfulfilled commitments, and too many shifts in priorities damaging the momentum of member engagement. Accountability begins to slide down, impeding the success of your organization. When members are not happy in the workplace, aren't personally invested in the organization and its objectives, and don't feel their work matters, they inevitably seek opportunities in another organization. This creates a vacuum of talent in your own organization. Filling that vacuum raises questions from candidates, like: "Why did my predecessor leave?" Answer these two questions in the space provided:

1. In what way does your organization actively pursue the retention of talent?

_____

_____

_____

_____

---

[77] Ibid., *Your Business Strategy Hinges on Employee Engagement*, 2020.

2. In what way does your organization actively engage its members?

_____

_____

_____

_____

Higher visibility in member engagement

The second reality is when member engagement positively impacts the success of your organization because it is directly related to responsibility, achievement, and accountability as I've defined in this chapter.

If it is that important—and it is—how can executive leaders raise the visibility of member engagement? Doing it yourself could be a little narcissistic. Well, there are multiple ways of doing this, but what is non-negotiable is visibility. Get creative. Answer the follow three questions in the space provided:

1. Should visibility be limited to the organization only? Whatever your answer, write down the reason.

_____

_____

_____

_____

2. When does visibility cross the line into becoming counterproductive?

_____

_____

_____

_____

3. Should the visibility of member engagement be celebrated? If so, how?

_____

_____

_____

_____

Summary

Review your answers to the questions in this chapter about agility and ask yourself if you really have the pulse of your organization. Are there measures in place to know the rate of adaptability, goals accomplished, achievements, and degree of member engagement? Do you agree that leadership can measure the four aspects of agility but cannot control the market environment that causes the organizational pulse to race a little? Reflect on your answers and journal some thoughts on how you can be more accountable in your role.

Now that we've come to the final chapter, let's talk about the future of your organization and the type of leadership that will take you there.

Part Three Conclusion

People are watching your organization. They are talking about it and asking questions. This can attract potential new hires to your organization. But believe me, they do their homework on you before they submit an application. So, "Shaping your culture is more than half done when you hire your team." Run through the nine steps that measure your interview process with your team and see if something is missing. It will not only inform them, but it will also clarify who you are as an organization.

> People are not only watching, but they are also measuring everything. You do work in a glass house even if the concrete walls are eighteen inches thick.

Hiring the right people is challenging, and you don't want the candidate to know more about you than you do the candidate. So, have regular updates in your organization that keep your people on the cutting edge of organizational identity. If asked, your people will tell you if there is evidence of discrimination through bias in your processes. Measuring your process from making an application to interview, and then to hire, will help you stay ahead.

People are not only watching, but they are also measuring everything. You do work in a glass house even if the concrete walls are eighteen inches thick. What people say about your organization is far more effective than paid advertising. People see, hear, and even touch your culture. If this is the case, part of your strategy must include in-house training that builds the culture through key performance indicators that intentionally track what's actually happening.

In the Austin Metroplex where I live in Texas, significant organizations have officed here. People want to work for Apple. Why? They want to work for Tesla. Why? They want to work for Microsoft, Amazon, Dell, eBay, Facebook, Google, Indeed, and many more. Why? All of these organizations have one common thread: they work hard at organizational culture.

They have the ability to remain agile by adapting to the present while predicting the future. Taking the pulse of any organization can be done in a variety of ways, but what is non-negotiable is the fact that you must take your organization's pulse rate.

Does that rate show your organization is adapting or panicking? Are you accomplishing goals and achieving them through excellent processes? Are you engaging all your members in those processes? Though agility can be measured, be sure of what you can control and what is out of your control. Who would have thought 2020 would put so many organizations out of business? Your organizational leadership can control the "corporate culture as the only sustainable competitive advantage completely within the control of leadership."[78] Do you need to tell your people, "Calm down" or "Let's pick up the pace"?

Once more, when you come to the end of this book, I want you to come back to your impressions in this section to see how those thoughts developed.

So, what comes to mind?

_____

_____

_____

_____

_____

_____

_____

_____

_____

---

[78] David Cummings, Cofounder of Pardot, 2011.

_____

_____

_____

    In the final section—and final chapter—of this book, I want to look at a growing phenomenon in leadership circles that is paving the way into the future: servant leadership.

PART FOUR

THE FUTURE

*"A leader is like a shepherd. He stays behind
the flock, letting the nimblest go out ahead,
whereupon the others follow, not realizing that
all along they are being directed from behind."*

(Nelson Mandela)

Vern Dosh, coauthor of *Wired Differently*[79] said, "I used to believe that culture was 'soft,' and had little bearing on our bottom line. What I believe today is that our culture has everything to do with our bottom line, now and into the future."

Remember what you read about the Dickensian world of the 1800s? How different our world has become since the days of a ruling class. Perhaps Dickens was trying to tell us something through the characters of Scrooge, Nicholas Nickleby, and David Copperfield who became, eventually, people who served others.

---

[79] Vern Dosh, Wally Goulet, and Tracy Finnman, *Wired Differently: How to Spark Better Results with a Cooperative Business Model, Servant Leadership and Shared Values*, Milner & Associates Inc., 2015.

Perhaps it was your grandmother who showed you the way or someone living on your street.

Whoever became your inspiration to lead through serving, this final chapter will help you with some practical ways to sharpen your skills as a servant leader. Leaders in organizations are fast becoming the servant leaders once imagined in novels, but now they are a widespread reality, or as Dosh said, "now and into the future."

CHAPTER ELEVEN

SERVANT LEADER REVOLUTION

Tim Cook said, "Ultimately, it's on the company leaders to set the tone...not only the CEO, but the leaders across the company. If you select them so carefully that they then hire the right people, it's a nice self-fulfilling prophecy."[80] After you have read through the material in this chapter, you will have a better understanding of how far organizational culture has come since the 1800s. Cook's simple and profound concept is to hire the right people who will hire the right people. So, I want to explore a recent phenomenon—even a revolution—gaining a lot of attention post-pandemic, particularly among startup organizations and new executives coming into established organizations: the servant leader. I want to ask this in three ways: 1) what does it looks like; 2) what does it take; and 3) what are the challenges?

> Servant leaders are revolutionary because they take the traditional models of the 2000s and 2010s—I mentioned in Chapter One—and turn it on its head.

What Does it Look Like?

Servant leaders are revolutionary because they take the traditional models of the 2000s and 2010s—I mentioned in Chapter

---

[80] Tim Cook, CEO of Apple, from *Business Insider*, March 19, 2015.

One—and turn it on its head. These leaders put members at the very top and serve them from the bottom up. Their attitude can be juxtaposed between serving and commanding, empowering and limiting, developing and curtailing, unlocking potential and stifling creativity, and brandishing authority. It's the mantra that Justin McLeod talks about: "I look for two things when I hire a new employee: ambition and humility."[81]

A servant leader moves beyond the transactional aspects of day-to-day business, and instead actively seeks to develop and align a member's sense of purpose with the organization. Servant leadership can also be considered a universal concept not limited to Britain and America. In organizations like schools, places of religious worship, corporations, startups, and non-profits you will find pockets of servant leadership all over the world. However, the root of this type of leadership is nourished in different soil.

Different soil, same roots

Regarding the East, servant leadership is rooted in Chinese philosophers from the fifth century BC such as Lao Tzu. He famously said that when a servant leader finished his work, the people would respond, "We did it ourselves."[82] It may sound like a hijacked statement, but a servant leader feels greatly rewarded when their team has accomplished something that benefits the organization. More so, the East is typically contextualized in collectivism.

Servant leadership in the West is rooted in the soil of religious conviction. The thirteen American Colonies were highly influenced by Protestantism, and much later the United States with Catholicism. Though it may be rooted there, the expression of servant leadership in the West is more socially aware than religiously. For example, Robert Greenleaf,[83] who wrote a groundbreaking book (for its time) on servant leadership became a movement. He

---

[81] Justin McLeod, founder and CEO of Hinge, 2020.

[82] Laozi. *Tao Te Ching*, CreateSpace, 2016, 17.

[83] Robert Greenleaf, *Servant Leadership: A Journey Into the Nature of Legitimate Power and Greatness*, Paulist Press, 2002.

was informed by the Judeo-Christian ethic, but practiced Quakerism. However, his servant leadership movement was clearly for all faiths or no faith at all.

If you have not heard of Greenleaf, think about Herb Kelleher the founder of Southwest Airlines who is frequently cited as the model of servant leadership. Putting members first resulted in a highly engaged workforce and thirty-five-plus consecutive years of profitability in the turbulent airline industry. Nevertheless, it still unnerves me that I cannot reserve a specific seat on their airline!

Answer the following three questions in the space provided:

1. In what way do the facilities of your organization demonstrate servant leadership?

_____

_____

_____

_____

2. Describe in a few words how the environment of your organization could improve its practice of servant leadership.

_____

_____

_____

_____

3. Who do you admire as a servant leader (even though that person may not be in your organization)?

_____

_____

_____

_____

What Does it Take?

Let's go back to Cook's statement about leaders hiring the right leaders who will hire the right people. The serve-first approach in a new hire can be put into practice from the beginning, and especially during their onboarding process. It's a hot topic and something that executives look for today: ambition and humility.

> The serve-first approach in a new hire can be put into practice from the beginning, and especially during their onboarding process.

Whether in an Eastern or Western context, what it takes for servant leadership to thrive is juxtaposed in two metaphors: robe and towel.

The robe of leadership

In the ancient Greco-Roman world, a robe was given to someone with special honor. Often, the robe signified an office, so the wearer could enjoy a kind of royal status with privilege, a name, prominence, and quite a few perks. We vividly see this in the time of Emperor Constantine (306-337) who included the Christian Church as a sanctioned religion. As such, the Church occupied facilities designed in basilica architecture, and with that, leaders of the church dressed like Roman senators in their robes. As a side, St. Augustine spoke out against the clergy in his day for their self-importance instead of serving the people. The clergy also received significant tax breaks that Augustine venomously spoke out against as a wrong motive to become clergy. I think you get the picture of the robe by now. A robe is not servant leadership.

The towel of leadership

Within the same Greco-Roman world, a radical young man called Jesus claimed to be the Son of God, and yet, washed his own team's feet.[84] So God washes feet? Apparently, yes. Ironically, Friedrich Nietzsche had nothing to say about this in his famous statement, "God is dead. God remains dead. And we have killed him."[85] Servant leaders, whether they hold to the Christian faith or not, defy Nietzsche in terms of the towel metaphor. In the world we encounter today, successful leaders care about their members in such a way that greatness is determined not by power over others but by service to people.

> Servant leaders love focusing on developing talent simply because they see others as the leaders of tomorrow.

Servant leaders love focusing on developing talent simply because they see others as the leaders of tomorrow. Leveraging the strengths of members with a view to relinquishing measures of power to run with projects are the delight of servant leadership. Andrew Mason, founder of Groupon, succinctly captured this approach when he said, "Hire great people and give them freedom to be awesome."[86]

---

[84] Bible, John 13:1–17.

[85] Friedrich Nietzsche, *God is Dead. God Remains Dead. And We have Killed Him*, Penguin, 2020.

[86] Gary Blair and Rusty Burson, *The Coaching Life*, Texas A&M University Press, 2017, 99.

Answer the following questions in the space provided:

1. Does your leadership look like a robe or towel? Write down the reason for your answer.

_____

_____

_____

_____

2. What would it take to relinquish your power to someone you are developing?

_____

_____

_____

_____

3. In what ways do your hiring and onboarding processes demonstrate servant leadership?

_____

_____

_____

_____

What Are the Challenges?

One of the biggest challenges is the idea that leadership equates to control. This idea is an antithesis to servant leadership. Members in positions of leadership who have a capacity to let go quite often discover they are in more control. It's a paradox. A servant leader knows how to harness the talent of their team and the resources available to them. As such, servant leadership collectively guides a project far more effectively than a single person. I think the "secret sauce" of servant leadership has two main ingredients: questioning closely and listening closely. Think about this—swimming and drowning look the same from a distance. However, when you get close to what is actually happening, you're able to rescue someone or enjoy the moment with them. Getting close is key.

> Members in positions of leadership who have a capacity to let go quite often discover they are in more control.

Questioning closely

Here are six questions to ask your collective team every month:

1. How can I be a better team leader?
2. What or who is missing from our team?
3. What can we do to improve our team culture?
4. What can we do to improve our product/service?
5. Is there a team-building activity we can plan for next month?
6. What can I do to better manage our team?

Write down two additional questions you could ask your collective team each month:

1. _____

_____

_____

2. _____

_____

_____

Here are six questions to ask the individual members of your team every month:

1. Looking back to last month, what is the one thing you would do differently?
2. Again, looking back, what is the one thing you are proud of accomplishing?
3. What are your biggest challenges this month?
4. What can I do to make next month more successful for you?
5. Is there any project you want to be involved in?
6. Is there any project you would rather not be involved in?

Write down two additional questions you could ask the members of your team each month:

1. _____

_____

_____

2. _____

_____

_____

The message these questions send to your team is that you want them to succeed individually and collectively. Over time your team knows these questions are going to be asked and will be more prepared to answer them, so you might want to change them up a little. It also creates a healthy environment for your team to ask you questions without feeling they are loading too much on your leadership plate.

Listening closely

Asking questions is one thing, but listening to the answers is something else. A servant leader will make brief notes because those details become useful when asking questions the following month. For example, if you asked, "What is your biggest challenge this month" and you helped that team member through the challenge, and the challenge still existed the following month, you may want to ask a different related question.

Basic listening comes down to three basic elements:

1. Not talking when others are speaking.
2. Letting the other person know you're listening through facial expressions and verbal sounds.
3. Being able to repeat what others have said, practically word for word.

However, you want to move beyond basic listening to great listening. The Harvard Business Review published four significant findings on what makes someone a great listener, far more detailed than the above three things.[87] What follows is an adaptation of their findings.

Semi-two-way dialogue: Great listening is much more than being silent while the other person talks. Listening is about periodically asking questions that promote discovery and insight. These questions politely challenge old assumptions that a team member many be leaning on. You do this in a constructive way. Silently nodding does not reassure the one speaking that you are listening. Asking a good question reassures you want to comprehend what is being said with additional information. So, great listening is seen as a semi-two-way dialogue, rather than a one-way speaker versus hearer interaction. The best conversations with your team will always be active.

---

[87] Jack Zenger and Joseph Folkman, *Harvard Business Review*, "What Great Listeners Actually Do," July 14, 2016.

Figure 11.1 Semi-Two-Way Dialogue

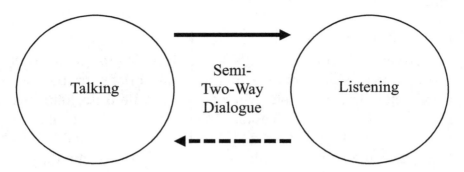

What are the challenges you may experience in periodically asking questions? Write your answer in the space provided:

_____

_____

_____

Building self-esteem: Great listening includes interaction that builds a person's self-esteem. Make it a positive experience for the team member. Great listeners make the other person feel supported by conveying confidence in them. Listening can be characterized by the creation of a safe environment in which issues and differences can be discussed openly.

Figure 11.2 Building Self-Esteem

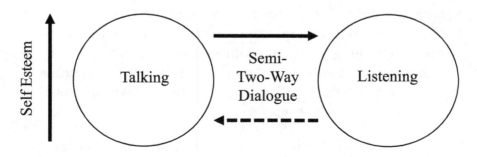

In what non-verbal ways can you inspire confidence in your team members that builds their self-esteem? Write your answer in the space provided:

_____

_____

_____

Cooperative conversation: Great listening is seen as a co-operative conversation. When you engage your team with great listening like this, feedback will flow smoothly in both directions with neither party becoming defensive about comments the other made. By contrast, poor listeners will be seen as competitive. This happens when listening serves the purpose of identifying error and correcting the reason or logic being used. This makes you an excellent debater, but it doesn't make you a good listener. Good listeners may challenge assumptions and disagree, but the person you are listening to will probably feel you are trying to win an argument. If so, the rest of the team becomes the audience which is always disastrous.

Figure 11.3 Flowing Feedback

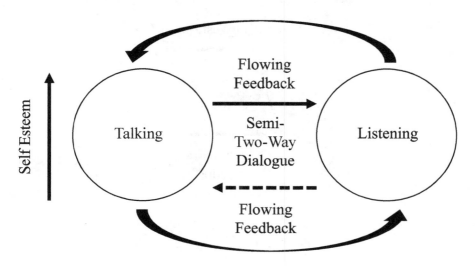

In what way can your conversation be cooperative? Write your answer in the space provided:

_____

_____

_____

Good suggestions: Great listeners tend to make good suggestions. Listening invariably includes some feedback provided in the way the one speaking would accept by opening alternative paths to consider. It's not uncommon to hear, "You didn't listen but just tried to solve the problem." So, making suggestions is not the problem but it may be the skill with which those suggestions are made. Someone who seems combative or critical and then tries to give advice may not be seen as trustworthy.

Figure 11.4 Great Suggestions

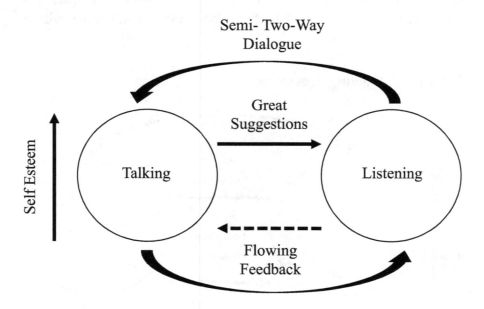

In what way can you defuse the idea that you may come across as combative or critical? Write your answer in the space provided:

_____

_____

_____

Summary

Tim Cook talks about a self-fulfilling prophecy when leaders hire the right leaders. At this point, I'm sure you can see the difference between the 1800's hierarchal ruling class and servant leaders today. Servant leaders have the same roots as other leaders, but the soil is more about serving than commanding. Figuratively, they carry towels but don't wear robes. They know how to lead. Question closely and listen closely. The skills for both come from a semi-two-way dialogue that builds the self-esteem of members through cooperative conversation. Review your answers to the questions in this chapter about servant leadership and ask yourself if you are this type of contemporary leader.

Conclusion

I would like you to write the conclusion! I'm not being lazy, I'm being engaging.

At the end of Section One I asked you to write down your first impression that came to mind having read a brief history of organizational culture from the 1800s to the present day. In what ways have those first impressions developed now that you have arrived at the end of this book? Write your answer in the space provided:

_____

_____

_____

_____

_____

_____

_____

_____

_____

At the end of Section Two I asked you to do that same thing with what came to your mind with a definition of organizational culture, hiring cultural fits, and keeping cultural adaptors. In what ways have those first impressions developed now that you have arrived at the end of this book? Write your answer in the space provided:

_____

_____

_____

_____

_____

_____

_____

Finally, I asked you to do that same thing with what came to your mind about measuring your interview process, performance indicators, and agility. In what ways have those first impressions developed now that you have arrived at the end of this book? Write your answer in the space provided:

_____

_____

_____

_____

_____

_____

_____

_____

_____

_____

Works Cited

Adams, Douglas. *Hitchhikers Guide to the Galaxy.* Pan Books, 1979.

Bernard, C. I. *The Functions of the Executive.* Harvard University Press, 1938.

Blair, Gary & Rusty Burson. *The Coaching Life.* Texas A&M University Press, 2017.

Bursztynsky, Jessica. MSNBC, May 22, 2020.

Cameron, K. S., R. E. Quinn, J. Degraff, and A. V. Thakor. *Competing Values Leadership.*

Egan, Jennifer. *Visit from the Goon Squad.* Knopf, 2010.

Elgar, Edward 2006.

Ellis, Brett. *American Psycho.* Vintage, 1991.

Carrick, Moe, & Cammie Dunaway. *Fit Matters: How to Love Your Job.* Maven House. 2018.

Chapple, E. D. *Organization Problems in Industry.* Applied Anthropology 1(4), 2-9. 1941.

Chapple, E. D. *Anthropological Engineering: Its Use to Administrators.* Applied Anthropology 3(1), 23–32, 1943.

Culture Partners. *Improving Employee Satisfaction Through Positive Accountability.* 2020.

Deal, T. E. & R. A Kennedy. *Corporate Cultures.* Addison-Wesley, 1982.

Dosh, Vern, Wally Goulet & Tracy Finnman. *Wired Differently: How to Spark Better Results with a Cooperative Business Model, Servant Leadership and Shared Values.* Milner & Associates Inc., 2015.

Gallup Poll. *U.S. Employee Engagement Rises Following Wild 2020.* February 26, 2021.

Gallup Poll. *Your Business Strategy Hinges on Employee Engagement,* 2020.

Gardner, B. B. *Human Relations in Industry*. Irwin Inc., 1945.

Gilbreth, Frank B. & Ernestine Gilbreth Carey. *Cheaper by the Dozen*. Thomas Y. Crowell, 1948.

Gouldner, A. W. *Wildcat Strike*. Harper & Row, 1954.

Grahame, Kenneth. *Wind in the Willows*. Methuen, 1908.

Greatness. Paulist Press, 2002.

Greenleaf, Robert. *Servant Leadership: A Journey into the Nature and Legitimate Power and Greatness*

Hickman, Craig, Tony Smith & Roger Connors. *The Oz Principle*. Portfolio, 2010.

Jacoby, S. M. *Employing Bureaucracy*. University Press, 1985.

Kihlstrom, Greg for *Forbes Magazine*, 2020.

Kilmann, R. H. *Five Steps to Close the Culture Gap*. In R. H. Kilmann, M. Saxton, and R. Serpa and Associates (Eds). "Gaining Control of the Corporate Culture." Jossey Bass. 1985.

Larson, C. E. & F. M. J. Lafasto. *Teamwork*. Sage, 1986.

Lawler, E. *Higher Involvement Management*. Jossey-Bass, 1968.

Martin, J. *Cultures and Organizations: Three Perspectives*. Oxford University Press, 1992.

Mathewson, Stanley B. *Restriction of Output Among Unorganized Workers*. Viking Press, 1931.

Melling, Maxine, & Joyce Little. *Building a Successful Customer Service Culture*. Facet Publishing, 2002.

Mitchell, David. *Cloud Atlas*. Scepter, 2004.

Moore, D. G. *Managerial Strategies and Organization in Sears Retailing*. Dissertation. University of Chicago, 1954.

National Research Council of the Academy of Social Sciences at the Western Electric Hawthorne in the publication of F. J. Roethlisberger and W. J. Dickson. *Management and the Worker*. Harvard University Press, 1939.

Neate, Rupert for *The Guardian*. "Starbucks Pays £18.3m Tax but £348m in Dividends." June 27, 2019.

Nietzsche, Friedrich. *God is Dead. God Remains Dead. And We have Killed Him.* Penguin, 2020

Ouchi, W. G. *Theory Z.* Addison-Wesley, 1981.

Palahniuk, Chuck. *Fight Club.* W. W. Norton, 1996.

Peters, T. J. & R. H. Waterman. *In Search of Excellence.* Harper and Row, 1982.

Pew Research. *Key Findings about U.S. Immigrants*, 2020.

Regini, M., J. Kitay and M. Baethge. *From Tellers to Sellers.* MIT Press, 1999.

Roethlisberger, F. J. & W. J. Dickson. *Management and the Worker.* Harvard University Press, 1939.

Trice, Harrison M. & Janice M. Beyer. *The Cultures of Work Organizations.* Pearson, 1992.

Tzu, La. Translated by Shalu Sharma. *Tao Te Ching.* CreateSpace, 2015.

Vanderbilt, Amy. *Complete Book of Etiquette: A Guide to Gracious Living.* Doubleday & Co., 1952.

Weitzman, Martin L. *The Share Economy: Conquering Stagflation.* Harvard University Press, 1984.

Whyte, W. F. *Pattern for Industrial Peace.* Harper and Brothers, 1951.

Wilkins, Eliza G. *Classical Philology.* 1927. University of Chicago Press. 22 (2): 121–135.

Zenger, Jack & Joseph Folkman. *"What Great Listeners Actually Do"* Harvard Business Review, July 14, 2016.

Noted Individuals

Agatha Christie (1890–1976), Author
Anne M. Mulcahy, CEO, Xerox (2001–2009)
Bob Parsons, Founder, GoDaddy Group (1997–2011)
Brian Chesky, Cofounder and CEO, Airbnb (2008–)
Brian Halligan, CEO, Hubspot (2006–2021)
Brian Kristofek, President and CEO, Upshot (1996–2022)
C. S. Lewis (1898–1963), Author and lay Theologian
Charles Dickens (1812–1870), Author
David Cummings, Cofounder Pardot (2007–2012)
David Mattin, Founder New World Same Humans (2020–)
Eliot Dismore Chapple (1910–2003), Anthropologist
Elliott Jaques (1917–2003), Psychoanalyst
Elton Mayo (1880–1949), Psychologist
Emperor Constantine (280–337)
Jessica Herrin, Founder and CEO Stella & Dot (2004–)
Jesus Christ (4BC–33AD)
Justin McLeod, Founder and CEO of Hinge (2011–)
Margaret Wheatley, Author and Teacher
Mark Parker, President and CEO of Nike (2006-2020)
Nelson Mandela (1918–2013)
P. G. Woodhouse (1881–1975), Author
Pausanias (110–180), Greek Writer
Peter Drucker (1909–2005), Management Consultant
Richard (1835–1899) and George (1839–1922) Cadbury
Simon Sinek, Author and Inspirational Speaker
St. Augustine (354–430)
Teddy Roosevelt (1858–1919), 26th President of the United States
        (1901–1909)
Tim Cook, CEO Apple Inc. (2011–)
Tony Hsieh (1973–2020), CEO Zappos (1999–2020)
W. H. Auden (1907–1973), Poet
William Foote Whyte (1914–2000), Sociologist
William Penn (1644–1718), Writer and Thinker

Invitation

You are probably asking, "So, what do I do about your organizational culture and where do I start?" Well, you have read the book, so you have already made a great start.

The good news is that Cultural Clarity is not just a book, it's something that I developed with my colleagues to help people like you grow your organization.

Here's your next steps.

Go to www.culturalclarity.us

Take the quick analysis test, it won't cost you anything except a few minutes of your time.

When you see the results schedule a one-on-one virtual meeting with me at no cost to you by clicking on "schedule your free call".

If you're serious about growing the culture of your organization our comprehensive assessment will give you the answers to those questions you're already asking.

And that's when you hire me.

I want to save you time and money, and help you grow your organizational culture, hire cultural fits, and help your existing members culturally adapt.

Go to the website and take the free analysis.

I'm looking forward to meeting with you.

andrew@culturalclarity.us

CPSIA information can be obtained
at www.ICGtesting.com
Printed in the USA
BVHW062351300522
638444BV00015B/756